Also by David Freemantle and published by Nicholas Brealey:

The Biz
50 little things that make a big difference
to team motivation and leadership

and

What Customers Like About You
Adding emotional value for service excellence
and competitive advantage

CONTENTS

THE
BUZZ

50 little things that make a big difference to delivering world-class customer service

DAVID FREEMANTLE

NICHOLAS BREALEY
PUBLISHING

LONDON   BOSTON

First published by
Nicholas Brealey Publishing in 2004
Reprinted in 2004, 2005, 2007, 2008

3–5 Spafield Street
Clerkenwell, London
EC1R 4QB, UK
Tel: +44 (0)20 7239 0360
Fax: +44 (0)20 7239 0370

20 Park Plaza, Suite 1115A
Boston, MA 02116
USA
Tel: (888) BREALEY
Fax: (617) 523 3708

http://www.nicholasbrealey.com
http://www.buzzandbiz.co.uk

ISBN 13: 978-1-85788-347-3
ISBN 10: 1-85788-347-0

British Library Cataloguing in Publication Data
A catalogue record for this book is available from the
British Library.

Library of Congress Cataloging-in-Publication Data
Freemantle, David.
    The Buzz : 50 little things that make a big difference to delivering
    world-class customer service / David Freemantle.
        p. cm.
    ISBN 1-85788-347-0
    1. Customer services. I. Title.
    HF5415. 5. F7267 2004
    658.8′12--dc22
                                                                2004012398

Printed in Finland by WS Bookwell.

ACKNOWLEDGMENTS

Writing a book is rarely a smooth process in which a solitary author produces a perfect typescript for automatic conversion into the perfect book. More often the end product has been improved substantially as a result of inputs from a number of team players who work behind the scenes to advise, cajole, and encourage the author to make changes for the better. It can be a difficult process and I must confess I am not the easiest author to deal with in this connection. It is easy to give advice but not to take it.

I thought I had written the perfect book until Nicholas Brealey, my publisher whose patience I must have exhausted, came along and struggled to convince me—the stubborn and difficult author—that the book could be even better. On reflection, he was absolutely right. I am duly indebted to Nicholas along with his excellent support team in the form of Victoria Bullock, Angie Tainsh, and Sally Lansdell for their helpful inputs and their forbearance in dealing with me.

My wife Mechi, as on many occasions previously, has been incredibly supportive during my extended absences at home and abroad while I researched and wrote this book (and its companion). She also made many helpful suggestions with regard to the text. I am duly grateful.

However, the prime inspiration for this book comes from the many "star performers" I have had the privilege of meeting around the world over recent times. These range from employees who have excelled in their performance at the front line to highly motivational chief executives who have a "switched-on," people-oriented and customer-focused approach that delivers results. Many of these people are mentioned by name in this book and I would like to thank each one of them for their inspiration.

INTRODUCTION

The buzz: Switched-on people

Organizations that provide world-class service "buzz." They are full of people who make a difference. These people are switched on and they get all the little things right. They seize every opportunity to please customers by going beyond the routine of everyday work. They put a spark into the way they do business and this ignites positive relationships that customers cherish. The spark comes in the minutiae of behavior, from the look in an employee's eyes to the words he or she chooses when speaking with a customer. The best companies aim to make every minute with a customer a high-quality minute and a totally positive experience that could not be bettered anywhere else in the world. When this is achieved a buzz is created.

Functional service: Switched-off people

When there is no buzz everything is flat. Employees are switched off and in turn switch off their customers. There is no imagination and no initiative. Procedures are followed and that is all. The service is minimal in every sense. Smiles are rare, indifference is the dominant tone, and attention is focused elsewhere, sometimes on costs, sometimes on tasks, sometimes on merely getting through the day. Everyone is unhappy and it shows. Mediocrity and ordinariness are the best descriptions of these organizations.

To understand why, it is worth spending a few minutes examining the history of modern customer service.

1982: The invention of modern customer service

Here is a confession. In my own book *Superboss*, which was published in 1984 and has been translated into 18 languages, not once did I mention customers or customer service. Before the early 1980s customer service was something to which few managers gave any thought. It was simply taken for granted. They assumed that it occurred and it was therefore not a focus for management attention, receiving little if any attention in management and business textbooks.

The concept of modern customer service was invented in 1982 by Tom Peters and Robert Waterman in their pioneering book *In Search of Excellence*. This stimulated people to focus on customers and service and not merely on production, industrial relations, and financial strategy.

Following the success of *In Search of Excellence*, virtually every organization in the world jumped on the customer service bandwagon and initiated customer service improvement programs. For example, during the 1980s British Airways transformed itself into "the world's favourite airline" by focusing on customers and initiating a series of improvement programs, starting with "Putting People First." Other companies such as Disney, Nordstrom, and Southwest Airlines became icons of progressive customer service, delivering as they did an exceptionally friendly approach in which empowered employees were motivated to deliver incredibly high standards of service. These companies literally buzzed with energy that not only attracted customers but also much publicity.

The 1990s: From customer service to CRM

But gradually the fashion for customer service changed into something different. During the 1990s it evolved into CRM (customer relations management). As companies struggled to reduce costs, improve efficiency, and enhance profits, they allowed technology and computers to take over many of the roles traditionally exercised by customer-friendly front-line people. Call centers, IVR (interactive voice recording), and internet ordering became the order of the day. Empowered front-line employees were proving just too expensive and too unreliable to provide cost-effective customer service.

Alienation of employees: The energy drain

The focus on technology, efficiency, cost reduction, and profit enhancement did not only alienate customers but also employees, many of whom went about their jobs with an attitude of total indifference to the customer. They saw themselves as commodities to be disposed of when times were tough and as a result took the sensible option: They walked away and joined other companies they thought would be better.

Even today, too many organizations still focus on the hard, impersonal side of their business. They become task driven and concentrate on numbers, targets, analyses, mechanisms, and processes.

Everything is systemized, even down to a scripted welcome and a procedure for railroading customers through a routine.

All this results in organizations that are "flat" and devoid of energy.

Examples of world-class companies that buzz

However, there are exceptions. These are the companies that have risen above the cold technology of CRM and modern customer service to create a buzz, a positive energy that radiates between customers, employees, and managers alike. These are progressive companies such as delivery service TNT Express, sandwich retailer Pret A Manger, Innocent Drinks, department store chain John Lewis, and progressive banks and financial institutions such as Birmingham Midshires and West Bromwich Building Society. Bettys and Taylors is another fine example. At its bakery in Harrogate, UK it has posters encouraging "Buzz buzz brainwaves" on which employees can write their ideas.

Singapore Airlines (SIA) also epitomizes a company that really buzzes. In the last few years I have flown with the airline more than 40 times with no bad experiences. Furthermore, I have yet to meet another passenger who has a bad word to say about SIA. Changi Airport in Singapore is by a long stretch the best airport in the world. It buzzes.

In fact around the world there are many companies that buzz, for example the retailer ODEL in Sri Lanka, Dhiraagu Telecommunications in the Maldives, and Rand Air in South Africa.

Managing the buzz: Emphasizing the soft side of business

In addition to their focus on profit, executives in these world-class companies put a lot of emphasis on the "soft" aspects of business management. Their highest priority is getting the people thing right. This means focusing on the psychology of the organization in terms of behavior, attitudes, relationships, motivation, communication, and how managers can radiate a positive energy that transmits its way through the structure to the front line and the interface with customers.

The ultimate outcome is a wide range of everyday behaviors that absorb this positive energy and in turn pass it on to customers. This is the buzz. Customers sense it as soon as they walk through the door or pick up the phone. They know that this company just hums with energy and that everything is going to go right for them. It is these little energized behaviors that can make a big difference in transforming a company into a world-class organization. Overall it requires people who are a little bit M.A.D., who can Make A Difference for customers.

How to use this book

The aim of this book is to challenge senior executives, managers, and front-line employees to focus on the little things they can do every day to have a big, positive impact on their customers. It does not seek to offer a prescription by way of "seven steps to success," but more a series of M.A.D. stimuli to each reader's own daily approach to customer service.

In the book you will find 50 little things you can do to make a big difference to your customer service and thus create a buzz. These 50 little things are separated into eight loose groups. The first of these are the "top ten" necessary to get you started. Then there are the "famous five" essential to getting the basics of customer service right. Other groups relate to foundation behaviors; the theater of buzz and the performance that goes with it; the little behaviors that are at the heart of the buzz; the little things you can learn through your own personal academy; and then, before a final five, some examples from the psychology of buzz.

I suggest you take a random dip into this book on a section-a-day basis, focusing each time on one simple thing (specified on that page) that you can do to make a big difference to deliver world-class service to your customers.

Training modules for the buzz

The book can also be used for those invaluable half-hour team training sessions that many companies and their managers hold on a daily or weekly basis. One suggestion is that a different member of the team selects one of the sections and champions the little thing that each team member can do that day to make a big difference for customers.

The buzz and the biz

Finally, as it is impossible to separate customer motivation from employee motivation and team leadership, readers might also want to acquire the companion volume to this book entitled *The Biz: 50 little things that make a big difference to team motivation and leadership*.

Forward to the basics…!

THE TOP TEN

This is a top ten of little things that world-class people do to make a big difference in serving customers. These top ten behaviors are consistently practiced on a daily basis and the impact on customers is positive, powerful, and profitable. Doing this gets companies recognized as being the best when it comes to service.

Wherever you work and whether or not you serve external or internal customers, you can start the buzz ball rolling by focusing initially on this top ten. Daily practice will take you a long way down the road of becoming a buzzing individual working for a buzzing company.

1   **Make customers feel special**

2   **Get the first five seconds right**

3   **Say something (create small talk)**

4   **Personalize interactions**

5   **Show you care**

6   **Make positive choices**

7   **Be curious**

8   **Create great memories for customers**

9   **Make a difference (be a little "M.A.D.")**

10   **Observe customers**

MAKE CUSTOMERS FEEL SPECIAL

Convert the ordinary into the extraordinary. Do something special for a customer today

Five extra words such as "Really nice to see you" can make a customer feel special. The sparkle in your eyes can have an equal effect. In fact, there are at least 100 opportunities every day to make customers feel special.

Before she had her baby, Charlotte Horne used to work in a call center in Leeds, UK. She comments: "Every evening as I went home I challenged myself to think of something special I had done for my customers that day. It's all about giving something extra to your customers."

Charlotte never saw her customers, only ever speaking with them on the telephone. On average she would take 80 calls a day, answering routine telephone enquiries and sometimes addressing problems that customers raised with her. What was impressive about Charlotte was that she loved going to work. She could not wait to pick up the first telephone call of the morning and throughout the day she looked for little things she could say or do to make her customers feel special. It might just have been a choice comment, or her warm friendly tone of voice, or grasping a particularly difficult problem and running with it to ensure a satisfactory solution.

Your buzz specialism is to make customers feel special

Charlotte was world-class at her job. She recognized that if you do little things to make customers feel special they will return to you time and time again. Everyone likes to be made to feel important, while no one likes to be made to feel ordinary. We are all unique and therefore we all believe we deserve unique treatment from the people to whom we give our custom.

Unlike Charlotte, many of us drift into routine and then miss out on hundreds of opportunities to make customers feel special.

The following are some guidelines for making customers feel special:

❖ Think special, feel special, and act special for all your customers.
❖ Keep the word "special" in your mind at all times and every time you encounter a customer seek to apply this word to your behavior with that customer.
❖ Try to identify the unique qualities in each customer and then do something unique to make them feel special.

Here are some further examples of little things you can do to make a customer feel special:

❖ Make some special comment, such as "I love your name, Maria. It's one of my favorites."
❖ Ask some special question, such as "I am intrigued by your accent. I hope you don't mind if I ask where you are from?"
❖ Do a special favor, such as "Just for you I am going to give you an upgrade on this occasion."
❖ Promise something special, such as "While our normal delivery time is seven days I promise I'm going do my best to get you the item delivered within the next 24 hours."
❖ Choose a special tone of voice that echoes an appropriate feeling, for example delight, or kindness, or excitement (depending on the situation and what the customer has to tell you).

By doing special things for customers day in and day out, you will become a very special person whom customers will seek out and bring their business to. This is the number one little thing you need to do en route to becoming world-class.

BUZZ PRACTICE 1
Hesitate for a brief moment every time you come into contact with a customer today, whether it be by face-to-face contact, telephone, email, or correspondence. During this moment think of a way you can make this particular customer feel special.

BUZZ QUOTE
Delivering world-class customer service is a specialism: making customers feel special.

2 GET THE FIRST FIVE SECONDS RIGHT

Ensure that a customer's first impression of you is positive.

The little things that go into the first five seconds are critical. All human beings have sophisticated sensing devices built into their genes. These are essential for differentiating friends from enemies, and also for distinguishing between safe opportunities and dangerous situations. Without them we become vulnerable and expose ourselves to undue risk.

These sensing devices are working at full stretch when customers move toward a potential service encounter. They will sense almost instantly whether the experience they are about to have will be positive or negative. They can tell by the look in a front-line employee's eyes, by the tone of his or her voice, by every microbehavior.

The first impression should never be the last impression

"I walked into a coffee shop yesterday," recounted Tom Gardner, "and knew instantly I was going to get bad service. There were a couple of empty tables, both of which were dirty and full of clutter. Behind the counter were three assistants chatting to each other and unaware of me as a customer entering the shop. When I ordered my cappuccino there was minimal interaction and hardly any eye contact. I asked them to clean one of the empty tables. They did so, removing the dirty cups but failing to wipe the spillage on the table or pick up the discarded napkins on the floor. It's the last time I will go there."

The "first five seconds impression" applies equally to telephone encounters. Within seconds of calling a company a customer can tell whether or not it buzzes with good service.

"I can telephone 20 different call centers," asserts Mary Callaghan, "and get 20 different responses. As soon as they try to railroad me through a set procedure I know I am going to get bad service. Before I open my mouth they are asking me for my account number, password, and other information. Yet on rare occasions I reach an individual who actually sounds like a human being. You can tell immediately by their friendly tone and their genuine interest in what I have to say."

If a customer's instant feeling is bad, there is a risk that they will walk away. The converse is obviously true: when customers detect a buzz they will want to stay and then come back time and time again.

Here are some little things you can do to ensure a perfect first five seconds:

✔ Step outside your premises and then enter as if you were a customer. What is the first thing you notice? Do people look up and smile as you come in? Is the floor clean? If you notice anything substandard during the first five seconds, take the necessary action.
✔ During your break call your company telephone number and ask for yourself. What is the first impression a customer would have on ringing that number? Is it easy to get through? Does the person answering sound friendly? Is he or she helpful? If the response is in any way poor, initiate the required improvements.
✔ Ensure that there is some positive engagement during that vital first five seconds as a customer approaches. For example, it could be a simple little signal with the eyes to indicate that you have acknowledged the customer's presence. Or it could be a nod or a little gesture with the hand.

The first five seconds can make a big difference to your business, but the challenge of getting them right is exceptionally demanding.

BUZZ PRACTICE 2
Today work hard with your colleagues to focus on the first five seconds with your customers. Role play encounters with customers where the first five seconds are absolutely fantastic—and then put your ideas into practice for real.

BUZZ QUOTE
The buzz starts with the first five seconds of any encounter with a customer.

3 SAY SOMETHING (CREATE SMALL TALK)

Initiate the relationship with ten words.

If you can't find ten words for a customer, that customer won't come and find you next time. So many front-line people have absolutely nothing to say to customers other than a robotic "Yes?" or "Can I help you?" or "Next?" supplemented by a minimalistic statement of the total price to be paid followed by a half-hearted "Thanks" and occasionally a muffled "Goodbye."

For example, in a retail store the customer hands the goods to a store assistant who scans the bar codes for the price, declares the total, takes the credit card, swipes it through a machine, indicates where the customer should sign, and then packs the items purchased into a bag. That is it. Nothing else happens. If it is a bank, the customer pushes the documents under the glass counter. The teller processes the papers and then pushes them back. Nothing else happens. If it is the reception of a large company, the receptionist will indicate to the visitor "Sign here," hand out a security badge, ring up for the visitor to be collected, and that is it. Nothing else happens. If it is an airline, the cabin crew will come round and ask "What would you like to drink?" or "Chicken or beef?" and that is it. Nothing else happens.

If you really want your place to buzz it is so simple. Say something! Create small talk! In one sense it doesn't really matter what you say, because whatever it is it will break the ice and warm up the relationship. Here are some examples, captured over recent times, of what front-line people who buzz actually say:

- ✪ "It's really hot today."
- ✪ "I think it's going to rain soon."
- ✪ "You're my first customer today."
- ✪ "I wish I was the man who invented paper."
- ✪ "You don't see many of these around now."
- ✪ "Let's use this till over here, it's my lucky till."

- ✪ "Thank you for being so patient and waiting."
- ✪ "You're in luck, this is the last one we have in stock."
- ✪ "My wife bought one of these and she's delighted with it."
- ✪ "I just love the design on the birthday card you're buying."
- ✪ "If I had to wait as long as you've been waiting I'd be very cross."
- ✪ "That's an unusual spelling" (observing how a customer's name is spelled).
- ✪ "You're obviously going to make someone happy" (customer buying a gift).
- ✪ "You're unique! This is the first time any customer has asked me that question."
- ✪ "It's Friday the 13th today. I believe that brings us all luck" (call center employee).
- ✪ "You can spend ten times as much on this type of product, but you couldn't do better than this economy version."
- ✪ "You look like you've had a good day's shopping" (observing a customer carrying many bags).
- ✪ "Sorry about the noise in the background, but there's some birthday celebration going on near me" (call center employee speaking on telephone to customer).
- ✪ "I am going to offer you a choice: small bag, medium bag, big bag, one bag, two bags, no bags. We have a lot of baggage in this business."
- ✪ "There are sixty ways to leave a lover but only six ways to leave this aircraft" (safety announcement by member of cabin crew).

Choose something to say

Silence breeds suspicion. When front-line people do not talk (other than grunting a routine response) customers do not know what is on their minds or in their hearts. So they assume the worst: "This person does not like me, care for me, want me here." Their perception is bad.

When front-line people say a few things they reveal their hearts and turn from robots into human beings. A buzz is created there and then.

BUZZ PRACTICE 3
Create opportunities to say things to customers. Try to find ten words or so for every customer you encounter. You will find that the relationship will build from there.

BUZZ QUOTE
Whatever you say to a customer beyond the routine transaction, it will break the ice and warm up the relationship.

11

4 PERSONALIZE INTERACTIONS

Add a personal note to every interaction with a customer.

Too much customer service is impersonal. The standard letter issued by a computer is impersonal. The scripted greeting provided by a call center is impersonal. The mechanical processing of a transaction is impersonal.

The Oxford dictionary definition of "impersonal" is pertinent here: "Not influenced by or involving personal feelings. Featureless and anonymous."

This could pass for a description of much of what we call customer service today. There is no feeling. It is featureless and customers are anonymous, mere numbers on a form.

The buzz can't be generated by impersonal, featureless, and anonymous systems. It can only be created by people who are personal with customers.

Being personal with customers means striving to know and relate to each one as a person. It means personalizing as much as possible of what you do for customers.

Delivering a personal approach to service requires giving something of yourself, perhaps a thought communicated, perhaps a piece of your heart or a soupçon of your spirit. Personalizing customer service allows customers to obtain a glimpse of the "real you" as opposed to the artificial system imposed by the company.

The act of personalizing service requires front-line people to take personal ownership of each interaction with a customer and thus accept responsibility for developing and progressing the relationship.

Every day there are hundreds of opportunities to personalize customer service and create a buzz. It takes time and it can be risky—but the benefit is that it might strike a chord in the life of a customer.

It takes very little to personalize an interaction. It could be as simple as adding a personal comment to a compliment slip rather than sending it out blank, or it could be starting an email with some appropriate and unique greeting that is specific to the customer. When you personalize an interaction the customer is more likely to remember you as a person than when the interaction is impersonal and devoid of feeling.

Here are some simple steps for personalizing customer service:

- ✪ Make yourself known personally to each customer ("Hello, my name is Zara, it's good to see you").
- ✪ Get to know the customer as a person ("I was just interested, Mrs Polson, do you live locally?").
- ✪ Do something personal to reinforce the relationship with a customer ("Mrs Polson, I've written my name here on the warranty, so if there's any problem just call and ask for me, Zara").
- ✪ Find a way of putting your personal stamp on the relationship, for example with a follow-up call ("Mrs Polson, this is Zara, I'm just contacting you to see if everything is all right following the purchase you made from us last week").
- ✪ Overall, show that you believe the person you are dealing with at the moment is the most important person in the world right now.

BUZZ PRACTICE 4
Practice personalization on a daily basis by adding a little of yourself to each interaction with a customer (internal or external).

BUZZ QUOTE
The choice is simple: Do you want your service to be impersonal (carried out robotically through procedures) or do you want it to be personal (identified with human beings who genuinely care)?

5 SHOW YOU CARE

Care is the essence of all relationships with customers. Convince customers that you care for them by demonstrating care.

Nothing alienates customers more than feeling uncared for. Most customers are tolerant when things go wrong. What they are less tolerant of is feeling that nobody cares about addressing their specific problem. It happens on many occasions, for example when flights are canceled, when the new computer fails to work, or simply when someone does not call back. The customer feels that no one is really bothered. This can apply to telephone companies, utilities companies, banks, and many institutions. Suddenly the customer is dealing with a large, faceless organization where nobody seems to care about their individual problem. They feel insignificant and helpless as a result.

Along with mutual trust and respect, nothing is more important in a relationship with a customer than genuine care. As soon as customers feel they are not being cared for, they will defect in their masses. When people care they genuinely desire the wellbeing of others (in this case customers) and are prepared to devote all their powers and energies as well as time to securing this wellbeing. Care relates to every aspect of business, for example taking care:

- ✔ To ensure that the product is delivered on time and not damaged.
- ✔ To ensure that a customer's problem is resolved quickly.
- ✔ To call back when promised.
- ✔ To be completely honest with customers.
- ✔ To communicate effectively with customers.
- ✔ To understand fully customers' real requirements.
- ✔ Not to rush customers (or make them feel rushed), thus allowing them time.
- ✔ To ensure that customers do not feel exploited and thus receive value for money.
- ✔ To assign customers the highest priority, thus overriding lower-priority, non-customer-oriented tasks.
- ✔ To ensure that the quality of the product or service is the highest possible in the circumstances.

By taking care you show that you care. Customers can sense when a person cares or does not care. It is reflected in every facet of attitude and behavior: in eye movements, in words, in tones of voice, and in actions. It happens when a taxi driver bothers to open the door for a passenger. It happens when a counter assistant explains that she is

having a problem at the till. It does not happen when a bank sends the same standard letter to all customers, irrespective of varying circumstances.

The sense of caring is a feeling, not a thought. You can only care for a customer if you genuinely care from the bottom of your heart. If you care more for something else, for example achieving your targets, or reducing costs, or getting home promptly at the end of the shift, this will show.

Care is reflected in everything you do for customers, while lack of care is not doing what, in the view of the customer, needs to be done. Customers will judge you by your demonstration of care or lack of it. They will know. You don't have to tell them you care. All you have to do is show them that you really do. It is all-pervasive and permeates every facet of the business.

So the challenge is to answer the question "Do I genuinely care for customers?" and if so, "Do I sincerely show this to them?"

BUZZ PRACTICE 5
At the end of every day spend five minutes with your colleagues and share stories of how each of you has cared for customers in the last 24 hours.

BUZZ QUOTE
To encourage employees to care for customers, bosses must care for employees. How can you expect front-line people to care if they don't feel cared for?

6 MAKE POSITIVE CHOICES

Every day there are an infinite number of customer service options. Always choose the positive.

Tony Chua was sitting in his favorite Starbucks at Millennia Walk, Singapore. He had retreated there to relax, drink a caffe latte, and read the *Straits Times* after a hard day at the bank's headquarters nearby. Suddenly a young waitress (or partner as they call them in Starbucks) called Eileen passed by to clean a table that had just been vacated. She knew Tony from previous visits. She turned to him and remarked, "I do like the tie you are wearing today."

Suddenly Tony felt happy. The waitress had brightened his day. As he reflected on her comment, it occurred to him that in the last ten years of sitting in cafés, hotel lounges, bars, and restaurants not once—ever— had any waiter or waitress complimented him on what he was wearing.

Eileen had made a positive choice, through a simple comment, to make him feel good. It came from her heart and she was genuine. Every day we are presented with an infinite number of opportunities to make such positive choices.

Eileen's team mates also make many positive choices that make customers feel good. As a result, customers like to go there. There are other cafés that Tony will avoid because the staff make him feel bad: they choose not to look happy, or they choose not to clean a table, or they choose not to make eye contact with him, or they choose to ignore him. He avoids these cafés. In fact, like all customers he avoids any establishment where people are likely to make him feel bad.

Whether a customer either feels good or feels bad invariably results from these little behavioral choices that front-line staff make. No matter how hard a company tries it cannot prescribe, through training procedure or customer service policy, the behaviors that employees must adopt in relation to customers. That choice is the prerogative of each employee and is driven by their own attitudes.

Here are some other examples of behavioral choices:

POSITIVE CHOICE OF MICROBEHAVIOR	NEGATIVE CHOICE OF MICROBEHAVIOR
Rush to open door for customer	Ignore customer walking through door
Raise eyes to make eye contact	Keep eyes down and avoid gaze
Greet unknown customer passing by	Fail to acknowledge passing customer
Warm tone of voice on answering phone	Automatic, matter-of-fact response
Personalize letter sent to customer	Rush off impersonal, standard letter

These little positive behaviors, if you choose them, will invariably lead to a buzz.

Here are some guidelines for helping you make positive choices:

✚ On your journey to work every morning, tell yourself you are going to choose to do some little things today that will have a positive impact on customers.

YES

✚ Throughout the day, look out for and create little opportunities for making positive choices.

✚ When in conversation with a customer, try to think of some little thing to say that is positive.

✚ When you have a spare moment, try to think of some little thing you can do that is positive.

✚ Do the same when your boss approaches.

✚ Get into the habit of reacting positively to everything you encounter at work.

BUZZ PRACTICE 6

When you arrive back home this evening (and every evening), sit down for five minutes over a cup of tea or coffee and reflect on the positive choices that you have made at work that day. If it helps, list them—even review them with your team mates tomorrow morning.

BUZZ QUOTE
When you choose to feel good about a customer, good things will happen.

7 BE CURIOUS

Be curious about all the little things you can do to make a big difference in the service you provide.

The founder of Dell Computers, Michael Dell, was asked what motivated him, given his success and wealth. "What motivates me is curiosity," he replied, "there is always a better way to do things. I choose to find them." He then explained: "With my savings I bought an Apple Computer when I was 15. I took it apart to find out how it

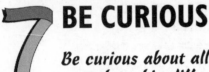

worked and realized I could make the computer better myself by buying my own components."

Nanz Chong-Komo, founder of ONE.99 shop in Singapore and winner of the International Management Action Award in 2001, says something similar: "I get insights into people's lives. Fifty percent of motivation is asking people how they are. Be interested in people first. Be curious."

Joe Howie, a partner working in the audio, television, and cameras department of the John Lewis department store in Newcastle, UK, regularly takes home new models of cameras and laptops in order to find out about their features. He effectively plays with them until he knows inside out how they work. His curiosity about new products enables him to give his customers the very best advice available.

Chris Hughes, one of the top independent financial advisers with the UK's Bradford & Bingley bank in 2003, is forever curious about new financial products coming onto the marketplace. He spends a lot of time finding out about the latest offerings so that he is able to give the very best advice to his customers.

Curiosity is akin to an open mind. People with closed minds are not curious. They think they know enough to get them by. Conversely, people who are curious want to know more so that they can improve themselves and the service they provide to customers. They realize that if they do not find a better way then someone else will and they will be out of a job.

The range of possibilities for being curious is vast. Be curious by discovering:

❖ What induced this customer to call your company.
❖ Why this customer is looking so angry.
❖ How this new product works.
❖ What motivates this customer.
❖ What are this customer's circumstances.
❖ Where this customer comes from.
❖ What type of product this customer normally uses.
❖ Why you have not seen this customer for a long while.
❖ How other companies provide such excellent customer service.
❖ Any national or international news that has an impact on your company's business.

Curiosity is a state of mind and a precursor to learning. People who are curious do little things like asking lots of questions. They therefore tend to get more answers than other people. In this way, they enhance their knowledge and race ahead in the competition stakes compared with those who rarely ask questions.

If something goes wrong, be curious and ask why. If another person is consistently successful, be curious and discover the reason.

Be curious about how to provide world-class service. If you persist in asking the questions you will obtain the answers and with suitable application you will become the best.

BUZZ PRACTICE 7
Be curious about things you don't know and don't understand. Ask ten new questions every day and put the answers to good use.

BUZZ QUOTE
Curiosity is the essence of success. It is all about discovering a better way to do things.

8 CREATE GREAT MEMORIES FOR CUSTOMERS

Anyone who is world-class is memorable. Be memorable!

Human beings are storytellers. Ever since the year dot families have sat down together over a meal and told each other stories: of encounters with others, of friends and foes, of fights and good fortune.

Despite email, text messaging, and the mobile phone, most people still like to socialize by sitting around and sharing such experiences. They are keen to learn what has happened to one another.

The memories thus created form the basis of relationships. When the memories are positive and powerful, the relationship buzzes. It is therefore important for employees to do little things for customers that they will remember and that they will want to tell their families and friends about when they get back home.

When the experience is bad and the memory lingers, there is always a high probability that a customer won't return. Memory influences choice and so influences the decisions that customers make. It is unlikely that we will return to a restaurant where we have a bad memory of our previous visit, for example. We are more likely to return to places of which we have good memories. Customers, like elephants, never forget.

Sharon Salehi, who works in customer relations for Bradford & Bingley bank in the UK, states, "I want every single customer who rings me to have a good memory of me when the call is finished."

Creating a positive memory requires unexpected action that registers in a customer's mind. When front-line people mechanically go through the transaction routine, their customers feel like numbers and can hardly remember the people who serve them.

So it is important to rise above the routine, to treat customers like human beings and do something special that will be remembered, like take a special interest in their particular circumstances.

No company can risk creating negative memories and this means avoiding any incident that alienates a customer. These often happen by default, for example when a customer is kept waiting for a long time without explanation or when a call-back is promised but does not occur.

The best protection against this is to initiate one or two good little things that a customer will remember. Here are some examples:

- ✔ Just be exceptionally friendly.
- ✔ Get back to a customer more quickly than he or she expected.
- ✔ Be bright and happy in doing your best to help, whatever the problem.
- ✔ Chat to a customer's children and take an interest in them.
- ✔ Take time out to help a customer with a specific problem.
- ✔ Share an interest with a customer.
- ✔ Follow up with a customer.

Who has a GREAT memory of you?

You might wish to recall your own recent experiences as a customer with various organizations over the last month. How many positive memories do you have? Compare these with the negative memories and those that are less than memorable.

BUZZ PRACTICE 8
Keep an informal log listing the things that you and your team do to create positive memories for customers. Review this list on a daily basis.

BUZZ QUOTE
The memories your customers have of your company will determine its future success or failure.

9 MAKE A DIFFERENCE (BE A LITTLE M.A.D.)

If you don't make a difference you will be the same as everyone else. Be interesting instead.

When you are the same as everyone else the chances of a customer choosing you are random. However, if you make a difference with all the little things you do for customers, there is a much higher probability that the customer will choose you. This means you have to be a little M.A.D.

When people follow routine they get into automatic mode. They close down their hearts and minds with the repetitive nature of their tasks. They cease to be themselves. As a result, they become tired and jaded and any sense of creative energy drains out of their work. When you can do your job "with your eyes shut," it probably means that you can't see opportunities for doing exciting new things that stimulate customers.

Rather than allowing yourself to become a clone of the system, it is important that every day you create a difference for customers by expressing your unique personality and being yourself. It is this difference that helps create the buzz.

Every customer is unique and if you treat them all the same the value in the relationship will be diminished. Customers will not feel special or important because you have not treated them as such.

Creative energy is thus essential in making a difference for customers. It means experimenting with new ideas that might stimulate a customer's interest and generate a positive experience. Customers are looking for such stimuli all the time. This is why they go shopping and take vacations. They want to get away from the routine and experience something new. It is a natural motivation. Your task in creating a buzz is to provide this creative stimulus for customers.

MAKING A DIFFERENCE

❖ Jim Dean, director of customer service at Saxon Weald Housing in the UK, received a poem of complaint from a disgruntled tenant. He composed a poem for his reply. The customer was delighted. In response to a request from customers, Jim also installed a water cooler in the reception area.

- Ruksana Kausa, when she was at Bradford & Bingley bank, received a complaint that a six-year-old child had not received the special offer promised. Ruksana personally selected some children's notepaper and wrote a handwritten letter to the child in reply. The child was delighted (as was her grandmother, who had opened the account on her behalf).
- At the EDSA Shangri-La Hotel in Manila, regular guests have their names engraved on coffee mugs so that when they return their own special mug is brought out for their coffee.
- At the Veranda Hotel in Grand Baie, Mauritius, the housekeeping staff make a difference by picking flowers from the hotel's gardens to decorate guests' towels in the bathrooms.
- Edwin Seah, a store manager with Starbucks in Singapore, organized a motivational picnic for his team. He invited some of his customers along too.
- Sharon Salehi and Mathew Jackson, from the customer relations team of Bradford & Bingley, organize a monthly "internal service award" for the best service provided to the team by another department.
- Annette Pampanella, a teller with Bank Atlantic in Florida, learnt sign language so that she could communicate effectively with a couple of customers who were deaf and dumb.
- Similarly, a team at Bettys and Taylors coffee shop in Harrogate, UK learnt sign language so that they could converse with a deaf-and-dumb colleague who had been hired.

The prize for making a difference goes to Rodney, a porter at the Palmar Beach Hotel in Mauritius. After each Saturday's soccer matches he memorizes all the scores and scorers. He does this for the UK Premier League and the other three UK divisions as well as for the Spanish, Italian, French, and German leagues. When guests arrive after an overnight flight, he chats to them as he carries their cases to their rooms. He asks which soccer team they support. "Southampton," one guest might reply. "You will be pleased to know that they beat Manchester United 1–0 yesterday and Beattie was the scorer." The hotel buzzes!

BUZZ PRACTICE 9
Become aware of all your routines and then step outside them. For example, move away from the scripted welcome to a unique personalized welcome that makes a difference.

BUZZ QUOTE
Make a difference by being yourself and doing little things differently from other people.

10 OBSERVE CUSTOMERS

Observe to serve and thus reserve your best for each customer.

By observing we learn what is going on and become sensitive to the nuances of customer behavior. This enables us to choose the appropriate moment to connect with them.

Human beings are very complex and emit a wide range of signals, often contradictory. These signals come in the form of basic behavior, body language, words used, tone of voice, facial expressions, general demeanor, and other patterns of movement. Unless we observe these signals and learn what they mean, there is a risk that we will misinterpret them or even ignore them. Poor observation will lead to clumsy interventions or a failure to intervene when required.

Skilled observation of customers requires immense reserves of energy. It is difficult. Our concentration can easily be lost and we can become distracted by the simple things that we would rather do. Carrying out a task often seems preferable to what many think is doing nothing: standing around and seeing what is going on.

Observing customers is far from doing nothing. By astute observation we apply effort to studying customers and determining their needs. Rather than remaining passive and waiting for a customer to ask us for something, through observation we can be proactive and get to customers before they get to (or get at) us.

Here are some useful observations:

❖ Observe the way customers talk to each other. You can pick up clues about when to intervene.
❖ Observe the way customers walk through your premises, what they look at and what they don't look at. This will give you an indication of what they are interested in and enable you to make a connection in conversation.
❖ Observe the way customers behave when sitting down with you: what they do with their hands (are they fidgeting?), what they do with their arms (are these crossed because they feel defensive?), what they do with their legs and feet (are they tapping their toes because they are bored?). All

these will create useful signposts for your behavior with customers and your response to them.

- ❖ Observe customers' eyes. These tell you a lot. Are their eyes on your face or over your shoulder?
- ❖ Observe what customers' children are doing. Often parents fail to observe and you can provide assistance by praising kids or preventing them from getting hurt.
- ❖ Observe any queues that form and use additional energy to manage the queue by signaling to people that you will do your best to be with them soon. Even one little nod on your part is sufficient to establish the relationship and keep the customer there (as opposed to having the customer walk out).
- ❖ Observe each customer's demeanor. Do they appear to be rushed? Do they seem to be interested? Do they appear simply to be browsing? Every piece of behavior will give you a clue to what to do next (if action is required) to meet that customer's need.
- ❖ Observe what the customer buys and the degree of interest taken in each purchase. These signals provide you with opportunities to make suggestions and help the customer.

There is always an appropriate moment for connecting with a customer, for saying something. Determining that moment is a fine art, however. Those who are less skilled rush in and approach customers too early, thus alienating them, while others leave it too late and annoy customers just as much. By observing customers and learning about their behavior, you can work out the best time to respond to their needs, to initiate contact, and in this way you can do your best for them.

To create a buzz you must be sensitive to what is going on around you. In this way you tune in to customers, to their emotions, their needs, and their requirements. To do so you must observe them.

BUZZ PRACTICE 10
Visit the front line with a colleague and observe your customers. Study their behavior carefully and discuss what you find.

BUZZ QUOTE
The more you observe what your customers are doing, the greater your opportunity to create a buzz.

10

THE FAMOUS FIVE

Basics alone = ordinary (same as everyone else)
Basics +++++ = big difference (world-class) = the buzz

To become world-class you have to go beyond the basics. But first, before you can even think about buzzing, it is necessary to get the basics right. Customers won't be impressed with any of the top ten little things you do (let alone any of the buzzing behaviors in the rest of this book) if at the same time they have to stare at dirty floors, experience delays, and put up with inefficiency. Your dynamism, energy, positive spirit, and relationship skills are wasted on a customer who can never get through on the telephone or has to wait a long time to get served.

The basics of customer service have been well documented elsewhere but are worth restating and reinforcing here—for the simple reason that even now many companies fail to apply them. The "famous five" of customer service are so important on the way to becoming world-class that there must be some measure of how well you fare on each of them. In the absence of such performance measures, no manager can control service delivery effectively.

11   First basic: Deliver as agreed

12   Second basic: Practice good manners

13   Third basic: Answer calls quickly

14   Fourth basic: Minimize wait times

15   Fifth basic: Follow up

FIRST BASIC: DELIVER AS AGREED

If you can't deliver what customers want, all the rest is fluff. Ensure that you deliver according to your agreement with each customer.

The first basic of customer service is that you must deliver. You can smile as much as you like, you can chat away and build relationships, you can do fun things—but in the end if you don't deliver the product to the customer at the agreed time the buzz will evaporate into thin air. It is like going to a restaurant where all the waiters are superfriendly but never get round to serving you the meal.

Creating the buzz is the advanced stuff. The beginners' course is to concentrate on the basics and the most important of the famous five is delivery.

This means that the product or service must be there when the customer wants it. Furthermore, it means that the product will be the one the customer wants, that the quality of stock picking is such that the customer does not get a skirt when ordering a shirt, and that the quantity is exactly right—two not one. In other words, it means virtually zero defects, or a "Six Sigma" approach to product quality and service delivery. There are too many stories of people having carpets laid that do not fit due to poor measuring and estimating, or receiving expensive furniture that has been scratched and damaged in the delivery process.

Given that our world is not exactly perfect, there will be occasions when things go wrong, when the delivery is not made or when what is delivered is not what was wanted. There are two essential practices for dealing with these situations:

1   You must inform the customer of the problem before he or she informs you of it.
2   You must have a recovery plan to resolve the problem. For example, when the kitchen runs out of chicken (or the chickens have run out of the kitchen), you must have some imaginative recovery plan for how best to respond to customers who ask for chicken.

When a customer discovers a problem before you do, the damage has already been done. If you identify the problem first you can take control of the situation and put yourself in the best position to manage the customer's expectations.

Here are some examples of little things you can do to ensure delivery:

✔ Assign top priority to delivery. Once a delivery commitment has been made, your top priority must be to ensure it is fulfilled.

✔ Flag all future deliveries to customers and double-check 24 hours before delivery that everything is in hand.

✔ Make a written note of everything you promise to a customer and review these notes regularly to ensure that you are delivering on your promises.

✔ When your promise to a customer is dependent on some action from a colleague, always politely check up that the action is taking place.

✔ If a truck breaks down, alert the customer that there will be a delivery delay, rather than having an angry customer call you.

✔ Similarly, if a consignment is held up in customs, inform the customer as early as possible.

✔ Ensure that the repair will be completed on time.

✔ Supply requested information to a customer within the promised hour.

✔ Mail the brochure today as promised.

✔ Process each insurance claim application within the specified two weeks.

Proactive communication is thus essential in ensuring delivery. Many experts would assert that a large degree of customer alienation stems from a failure to communicate properly. Being world-class means that not only do you deliver, but you take the extra little step of keeping the customer informed about the delivery.

BUZZ PRACTICE 11
Every employee should be 100% clear about exactly what they are expected to deliver in the job; to whom it should be delivered (exactly who the customer is); when it should be delivered; where it should be delivered; and the quality standard with which it should be delivered.

BUZZ QUOTE
Delivery is the first of 50 little things necessary to become world-class.

12 SECOND BASIC: PRACTICE GOOD MANNERS

Ensure that the manner in which you serve a customer is good.

"Teaching your grandmother how to suck eggs" is not exactly good manners, but this chapter is exactly that. While it might be obvious that the practice of good manners is necessary for good service, we all have recent experiences where this has not happened, where front-line employees have not bothered, have been disinterested, ignorant, or rude. Unfortunately, we live in a world where good manners are being eroded, where people don't reply to emails, fail to call back, and occasionally fail to show up without explanation. Many people don't even say thank you.

Good manners is as simple as being polite and courteous. It means treating all customers with respect and dignity. There is nothing complicated about this. It is the basis of any civilized society.

Here are some good manners and common courtesies:

1 Being punctual
2 Saying thank you
3 Making way for people
4 Opening doors for people
5 Answering letters promptly
6 Calling back when promised
7 Maintaining a good appearance
8 Offering to carry someone's bag
9 Being polite and courteous at all times
10 Giving compliments whenever possible
11 Keeping people informed of what is going on
12 Refraining from interrupting people
13 Listening carefully to what people say (and paying attention)
14 Offering refreshments (even a glass of water) at the appropriate time
15 Asking people how they are (with many personal variations on this theme)
16 Saying please
17 Replying to all emails
18 Offering someone a seat
19 Extending a helping hand
20 Extending a warm welcome
21 Pouring tea for a customer
22 Offering to take someone's coat
23 Saying goodbye when someone leaves
24 Standing aside to allow others to go first
25 Showing people to the door when leaving
26 Looking people in the eye when speaking
27 Volunteering to do something a customer is trying to do
28 Turning off mobile phones in meetings
29 Never being rude to anyone (e.g., an unkind remark or a nasty look)
30 Ensuring everyone in a small group is introduced to one another

Even recently, when I was at lunch with a client, the waiters scored less than 40 percent on the above list. No doors were opened, there was no warm welcome, there was no offer of help with the menu, there was no interest in whether or not the meal was being enjoyed, and finally there was no goodbye on leaving.

In fact, nobody noticed we were leaving. Then to cap it all—two weeks later as I revised this section—I recalled that I paid for the lunch and so far have received no thanks from the client.

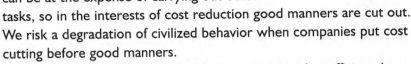

Good manners are absent in many establishments for the simple reason that they get in the way of so-called efficiency and carrying out the jobs set by managers. Opening doors for customers takes time and can be at the expense of carrying out other tasks, so in the interests of cost reduction good manners are cut out. We risk a degradation of civilized behavior when companies put cost cutting before good manners.

The practice of good manners might appear grossly inefficient, but ultimately it is immensely rewarding. The payback is immeasurable. The core of good manners is respect for other people, and money can't buy respect.

BUZZ PRACTICE 12
Review the list of 30 good manners above and, working with your colleagues, revise it as you think appropriate. Then use it as a checklist to audit your practice of good manners with customers (internal and external) today.

BUZZ POINT
Good manners are good for business.

12

13 THIRD BASIC: ANSWER CALLS QUICKLY

Pick up that ringing phone now. Never allow any phone to ring for longer than five seconds.

A five-second telephone response received early fame in the lexicons of customer service practice. That's sadly where it seems to remain—in the annals of customer service history. One of the near impossibilities of current customer service practice is trying to reach many companies on the telephone. Nothing can irritate a customer more than when the phone rings and rings and no human being answers. Companies can spend millions on marketing only to squander it through a failure with telephone responses. Even when I was writing this chapter, I tried to ring a locksmith who had a full-page advertisement in *Yellow Pages*. After 20 rings I gave up. The locksmith who got the business (Access Locksmiths Ltd of Southampton) answered immediately.

There are some progressive companies that do get it right. For example, TNT Express has a clearly stated telephone policy. One of its salient features is that there should be no telephone screening.

The frustration of trying to reach a human being by telephone has partly been offset by the proliferation of cellphones. If customers are lucky enough to obtain the mobile number of their prime contact in a company, there is a better chance that person will talk to them—even at the expense of the people he or she is having a face-to-face meeting with. However, this is only applicable when a relationship has been established between a customer and someone within the company.

The time has come to remove the barriers of access to a company and to eliminate the waste of time and frustration suffered by millions of customers in trying to reach a human being in order to get their classified advertisement placed, their broadband connected, their computer mended, their copying machine serviced, their refrigerator repaired, the pothole in their sidewalk filled, their flight plan changed, their hotel booked, their insurance policy explained, their magazine subscription canceled, the query on their car lease answered, the wedding gift for their niece ordered, or the light bulb at the crosswalk replaced.

Addressing strategic issues relating to staffing levels for telephones, productivity targets, and cost-effectiveness might be beyond the reach of many readers. Even so, there are some little things that everyone can do to ensure that as many calls as possible are answered quickly:

- ✪ Always pick up and answer a ringing telephone, even if it isn't yours.
- ✪ If you can't address the issue there and then, ensure that you follow up on the call and that the person the customer wanted to speak to calls back.
- ✪ Encourage your colleagues to work to the discipline of putting their phones on divert whenever they leave their desk.
- ✪ If you work in a call center and too many customers are becoming frustrated with the length of response time, put pressure on your managers to improve staffing levels. Why should you take all the flak from irate customers who have been hanging on for a long time?
- ✪ Create a game with your colleagues so that there is a penalty for any phone ringing on your floor for longer than ten seconds.
- ✪ Initiate a "forward to the basics" campaign that focuses initially on ensuring a five-second telephone response throughout the company (for both external and internal calls).
- ✪ Draft a telephone policy for your department (or possibly company) that incorporates world-class telephone practice—and then pioneer it yourself.

Be the first to answer the phone. And be the first to initiate a campaign to move forward to this famous basic of customer service.

BUZZ PRACTICE 13
When away from the office, try posing as a customer and ringing yourself. Can you get through to your company's switchboard in five seconds? When the call is put through to your extension, does someone pick up your phone within five seconds?

BUZZ POINT
Keeping the customer hanging on is a value statement. It says: "Your time is less valuable to us than that of our employees."

14 FOURTH BASIC: MINIMIZE WAIT TIMES

Why make customers wait when most businesses are just waiting to steal your customers? If you see customers waiting today, drop everything to serve them.

In this highly competitive world, most companies find it incredibly tough to attract customers. It requires a great deal of ingenuity and hard work to persuade customers that they should give you their precious money in exchange for goods and services. It is therefore madness of the highest order, having invested thousands (if not millions) to get people to walk through the door with the intent to purchase, for them to find that they can't do so—because they are kept waiting.

No wonder that people walk away and channel their money elsewhere. No wonder that so many companies go out of business. During my seminars I often invite my audience to raise their hands if they have ever walked out of a place because they have been kept waiting. Most people do.

The pressures of everyday life are such that time is increasingly precious. Few of us can afford the time to stand around in lines twiddling our thumbs and feeling irritated.

The longer customers wait, the shorter the time they will be with you.

As discussed in the previous chapter, keeping customers waiting simply indicates that their time is less precious than that of your employees, and that you are prepared to squander your customers' time in order to make maximum use of your employees.

Visit most banks and you will see evidence of this. There might only be two counters open, with a long line of patient (sometimes impatient) customers waiting to be served—and meanwhile there are large numbers of so-called back-office people flitting around behind the scenes, preferring to shuffle paper and complete the bureaucracy rather than attend to customers who have to rush to school to pick up their children, or get to the hospital for an important visit, or purchase essential items at three other stores.

If your company really does want to create a buzz, there are many little things you can do to prevent customers waiting too long:

✔ Stop any idle chitchat.
✔ Drop everything to serve waiting customers.
✔ Summon your colleagues to open additional counters.
✔ Pull people away from their back-office paperwork to serve customers.
✔ Drag managers out of meetings so that they can serve customers too.
✔ Inform the waiting customers that everything possible is being done to serve them quickly.
✔ Ensure that every person in the company has the skills and know-how to serve customers at the front line, so that when a flood of customers pours in there is ample back-up reserve to deal with them.

These guidelines are simple and rather basic. But if you don't follow them you will find that customers will increasingly exercise their own choices. Rather than wait they will walk away from you, your company will go out of business, and you will be out of a job.

BUZZ PRACTICE 14

If you work in an environment where customers come face to face with you and your colleagues, set yourself a goal, today (or perhaps tomorrow), of having a "no wait day." Try it out and see what happens. Just focus all your energies, all your people, and the whole organization on ensuring that customers don't have to wait when they walk through the door. See what happens. Then try it again at peak periods.

BUZZ POINT
Wait on customers rather than making them wait for you.

14

15 FIFTH BASIC: FOLLOW UP

The end of the transaction is not the end of the relationship. Follow up with customers.

Too often customers buy something and that is it. They disappear, never to be seen again. Nothing has happened except for an exchange of money for a chosen purchase. End of story. End of any opportunity to follow through and build relationships, let alone generate sales. One estimate is that an additional 20 percent revenue can be generated through effective follow-up.

While most companies obviously want to increase their sales, the purpose of the follow-up is not to force a second purchase from a customer. It is to develop the relationship by determining whether or not the customer is happy with the item recently purchased, whether any problems have been encountered, and generally to obtain feedback from each customer about their experience of using the product.

Here are some little things you can do to follow up:

✔ For all big-ticket purchases, call the customer after a week and then again after three months.
✔ For small-ticket purchases call a random selection of customers the day after the transaction.
✔ Use at least half an hour of off-peak time each day to follow up with customers.
✔ Devote the occasional evening to following up with customers who are not available during the day.
✔ Send a follow-up note, card, letter, or email immediately after a purchase.
✔ Working with the team, call up your colleagues' customers on their behalf and vice versa (it is important that a customer relates to more than one person).
✔ Invite the customer to an event that your company is holding.

One major international telecommunications company encourages its board directors to phone at least three customers every day. The customer services department provides them with a list of all customers who have called the previous day and each director randomly selects at least three customers for follow-up calls on how the initial call was handled.

The follow-up need not necessarily wait until the customer has disappeared. It can be as simple as a waitress asking with genuine interest: "How did you find your bowl of laksa? Was it too spicy for your liking?"

Here are some further examples:

✪ "Good afternoon, Mrs. McGregor, this is Jake from the insurance company. One of my colleagues, Debbie, recently settled your claim for damage caused by a burst water pipe. I'd be keen to receive your feedback about how we dealt with the claim."

✪ "Good morning, Mr. Simpson. I'm Hanif from the computer store and you bought your new laptop last week from me. I just want to know how you are getting along with it and especially the new Bluetooth remote control for your presentations."

✪ "Mrs. Chaudry, this is Megan from the travel agency. You will recall that my colleague Charmaine and I arranged your recent stay at the Heritage Hotel in Bel Ombre, Mauritius for you. I'm keen to learn how you enjoyed it, as I've had quite a few enquiries about that specific vacation recently."

✪ "Mr. Singh, I hope you don't mind me sending you this little note, but I would just to like to thank you for your custom yesterday, and your patience when I was urgently called away. I do hope Mrs. Singh likes the watch you bought for her when she returns from New Delhi."

✪ "Mr. Isaac Rapuli, forgive this short email but I wanted to let you know it was a great joy to meet you yesterday. I am sure your daughter Annah will be thrilled with the doll you bought for her. She looked such a lovely girl in the photo you showed me."

By following up you show customers that you and your team are genuinely interested in the purchases they have made and their experiences, and furthermore keen to help with any additional service information, advice, or action required. You also provide reassurance that there is a willing team available to provide support when needed. By reinforcing the relationship in this way you put yourself in the best position to obtain additional sales when the customer is next in need.

BUZZ PRACTICE 15
Initiate a team campaign to follow up with customers so that each customer has a relationship with more than one member of the team.

BUZZ POINT
The more you follow up with customers the more
they will follow you.

37

THE BUZZ FOUNDATION

There is much research evidence showing that companies that are successful over a long period of time are driven by a foundation of principles, values, and beliefs that are applied consistently in everything they do. The people in these companies live and breathe these principles. This is reflected in all the little things that make a big difference to customer service on a day-by-day basis. Such consistent practice generates the trust that is so essential in building world-class customer relations.

Companies that lack this foundation of principles tend to be expedient and blow with the wind. They are inconsistent in their approach because they have no guiding force. As a result, they are often viewed with suspicion, as neither customers nor employees know where they stand.

All the little things you do to create a buzz and make a big difference must therefore be checked resolutely against these principles.

16   **Be totally honest and open**

17   **Be hospitable**

18   **Be flexible**

19   **Give customers the benefit of the doubt**

20   **Be generous with customers**

16 BE TOTALLY HONEST AND OPEN

Tell the truth at all times and let customers know what is going on.

One of the most common complaints from customers is that they feel they have been misled by a company that has not come completely clean with them, for example about additional charges, stock levels, delivery schedules, or the quality of the product. Another aspect is the notorious "small print," where companies attempt to divert customers' attention away from critical information.

A further common example is a lack of honesty and openness in the selling process. Eager to close a sale, the salesperson will frequently neglect to mention potential problems with the product. There is a natural tendency to put a gloss on everything and show off products in the best possible light. No one wishes to hang out their dirty linen in public. Nevertheless, the honest and open truth is that dirty linen does exist and customers will feel let down if they discover it too late. They need to know the bad points about what they are purchasing as well as the good aspects.

Being totally honest and open with customers is absolutely critical if meaningful relationships are to be built up over a long period of time. As soon as a customer perceives a lack of honesty and openness, trust will be eroded and there is a high probability that the customer will disappear.

The following are some little things that reflect honesty and openness:

- ✪ Keeping customers informed all the time.
- ✪ Not hiding bad news from customers (e.g., a delay).
- ✪ Pointing out critical clauses in the small print of a contract.
- ✪ Accepting and declaring responsibility (e.g., for damage) rather than blaming anyone else.
- ✪ Drawing customers' attention to product limitations and potential problems.
- ✪ Providing a balanced view (rather than a one-sided or exaggerated opinion).
- ✪ Simply telling the truth about stock levels, delivery times, etc.
- ✪ Avoiding excessive flattery.

The buzz can only exist when there is trust and customers feel confident that they will be receiving the real thing. Employees feel bad when they have to cover up and make excuses for their company. The buzz burns off fairly quickly when this happens.

One of the little things that each of us can do every day is to challenge the way we communicate with customers. We simply need to ask ourselves the question: "With respect to the current transaction with a customer, am I communicating in an open way so that he or she knows everything necessary about what is going on?"

Failure to ask this question will lead to a communication vacuum and the spread of suspicion. Filling the vacuum requires a high degree of sensitivity to customers' needs for communication, together with a proactive mentality and an investment of time and effort to keep customers informed.

Another way of looking at this is to ask ourselves a further question: "If I were the customer, would I be satisfied with the information being provided? Is this person being totally honest and open with me?"

BUZZ PRACTICE 16

Test your conscience: "Am I totally honest and open with my customers?"

If the answer is "yes," verify this by asking your customers (using a survey or follow-up telephone call seeking feedback).

If the answer is "no," address the issue immediately.

BUZZ QUOTE
Trust is the cornerstone of all relationships and is built on total honesty and openness.

16

17 BE HOSPITABLE

If you believe in friendly service, behave toward customers in the way you behave toward your friends.

Hospitality embraces a warm and friendly reception for all visitors to your premises so that they feel comfortable and are at ease on entering your building. It means being delighted to see visitors and helping them overcome any problems they might have encountered in bringing

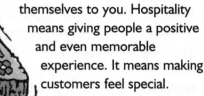

themselves to you. Hospitality means giving people a positive and even memorable experience. It means making customers feel special.

Jane Hume, personnel director of a chain of chicken restaurants in South Africa, says: "We dare our staff to make the customer a friend." Asked what she meant by this, she replied that the use of the term "friendly customer service" begged the question of what we mean by a friend. A friend is someone we like to see, with whom we like to spend time, whose company we enjoy, whom we can trust, to whom we can take our problems.

Hospitality embraces friendship. It means presenting yourself to your customers in an open and delightful way. It means being pleased to see customers as well as hear from them. It means putting yourself out for them.

Here are some examples of how the principle of hospitality can be converted into practical behaviors:

- ✪ Greeting a customer at the door.
- ✪ Introducing a customer to your colleagues.
- ✪ Offering to take a customer's jacket and hang it up for him or her.
- ✪ Pulling up a comfortable chair for the customer to sit on.
- ✪ Offering a customer a cough candy if he or she starts coughing.
- ✪ Presenting the customer with a small gift, even a candy or a cookie.

You can start practicing being hospitable with members of your own team, perhaps using some creative role plays in your weekly half-hour team sessions.

Hospitality not only relates to the hospitality trade (hotels, tourism, travel, conferences, and events) but to all industries, including banks, retail, engineering, public sector, and charities.

It might sound like a truism, but the better the hospitality you provide to your customers, the better the service will be. You should avoid the reverse syndrome, which is to drain your costs so much that there is no scope for even minimal hospitality. What is the cost of a welcoming cup of tea in winter or a glass of juice in summer?

HOSPITALITY GUIDELINES

✔ Hospitality must be genuine. It must come from the heart.

✔ Hospitality must be spontaneous.

✔ Hospitality is a function of people's attitudes, not of corporate policy and procedure. It is not a function of money, or of costs or budgets. Hospitality reflects the ethos in your organization: that you receive customers warmly.

✔ Hospitality (in its worst sense) should never be used as a bribe or an incentive. It is not something you "trade" to secure business from a customer.

✔ Hospitality should be applied to every visitor, irrespective of status or importance (in other words, don't reserve hospitality for VIPs).

BUZZ PRACTICE 17

Create a buzz today by focusing on hospitality and demonstrating it to every customer (internal or external) who enters your department.

BUZZ QUOTE

Do you really want to work for an organization that is inhospitable to its customers? Hospitality is not a waste of time and money but an essential investment in building buzzing relationships.

18 BE FLEXIBLE

Be prepared to break the rules and bend the system in favor of customers.

While on assignment abroad Sharon Tan, a trainer with a computer company, went shopping at a local supermarket to pick up a few grocery items to keep in her hotel room. When she went to pay, she found long lines of customers waiting at each counter. Then she noticed two "fast track" checkouts where no customers were waiting. The checkout sign said: "Fast track: for 10 items or less." As her basket was not too heavy, she went to one of these empty counters. The assistant looked at her with a frown and asked her how many items she had in the basket. Sharon didn't know, she hadn't counted them. He then began digging through her basket, counting each item. He discovered, as she feared, that she had 12 items. Instead of a three-pack of yoghurts (which would have counted as one item) she had three individual yoghurts. The assistant reprimanded her and told her she would have to go and queue at one of the other counters. At that point Sharon left her basket on the counter and walked out. She hurried to the 711 shop nearby, where she had no such problem. She will not return to that particular supermarket.

While it is essential to have rules, it is also essential to flex them from time to time if it makes sense. The risk is that when you comply rigidly with the rules customers become alienated. Rules are designed to help serve customers.

Here are some other illustrations of where you can be flexible in creating a buzz for customers:

✪ Opening the doors (to the bank or store) before the official opening time when customers are queuing outside in the rain.
✪ Not keeping strictly to warranty deadlines. For example, not charging a customer for a repair if the product is returned one day after the one-year warranty expires.
✪ Providing service at the table when the rules say self-service.
✪ Rounding down the price. For example, when the bill adds up to $11.05 only charging $11.00 and letting the customer off five cents. (In certain countries like Cyprus this happens frequently.)

✪ Giving the customer extra. For example, giving the customer a large portion when they have ordered a medium one.

✪ Agreeing to compensate a customer who is demanding the cost of a train fare for returning a defective item, even when the rules don't permit this.

✪ Allowing three people to visit a patient in a hospital ward when the rules only permit two, and permitting visitors outside official visiting hours (provided that they don't interfere with nursing and medical treatment).

✪ Allowing some deviation from the specified special offer.

✪ Giving clients more time than they have been charged for.

✪ Extending opening hours for the benefit of customers ("No problem if you can't come in before 5.30 p.m., we'll keep the doors open and wait for you").

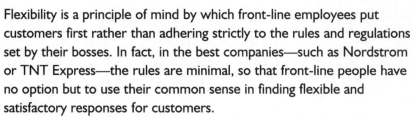

Flexibility is a principle of mind by which front-line employees put customers first rather than adhering strictly to the rules and regulations set by their bosses. In fact, in the best companies—such as Nordstrom or TNT Express—the rules are minimal, so that front-line people have no option but to use their common sense in finding flexible and satisfactory responses for customers.

Flexibility means training people to exercise their judgment without fear of retribution from their bosses if a rule is broken. In the end there is only one rule, which obviously is: "Do your best to please customers."

BUZZ PRACTICE 18

Review your rules for serving customers and explore the boundaries that could be broken. In other words: "If this happened, how far could we go in breaking the rules?" If both the customer and the company benefit from a flexible approach, the answer speaks for itself.

BUZZ QUOTE
When rules relating to customer service are unbreakable they will break the company.

19 GIVE CUSTOMERS THE BENEFIT OF THE DOUBT

Don't treat customers like criminals.

When Violet Parker, a senior citizen, returned a damaged new blouse to the department store where it was bought, she was asked for the receipt. Being rather absent-minded she had unfortunately lost it, although she clearly remembered buying the blouse from that store. The assistant gave her the benefit of the doubt and exchanged the blouse for a new one.

Most customers are honest and would be loath to exploit a company's goodwill. It is therefore unwise to create policies that put customers through rigorous interrogation when they are in pursuit of their rights, for example with respect to refunds and exchanges. The majority of customers can be taken at their word and should not have to prove, with explicit evidence, what they are claiming.

So never doubt a customer unless you have rock-hard evidence that he or she is lying or wrong. When a customer returns a product and states "I bought this here yesterday and when I got it back home I found it was broken," you should replace the item instantly and with delight, unless you are absolutely sure that the customer damaged the product.

Similarly, if a customer complains that she has been overcharged you should refund the difference instantly, unless it is perfectly clear that she has mistakenly put the decimal point in the wrong place in her calculation.

In most cases (although not all) it is not worth the hassle of arguing with customers who are convinced they are right and you are wrong. You will gain much more mileage if you humbly admit your mistake and allow customers to benefit.

Doubt is just that: it is not certainty. When you are certain that the customer's demand is unjustified, it is obvious that with politeness and courtesy you should turn it down. This is why it is erroneous to assert "The customer is always right." Sometimes the customer is wrong.

The danger is that we go around with an attitude of suspicion all the time. This is fostered by senior executives who generate policies, rules, and regulations based on the concept that customers are rogues. They argue that these restrictive policies are necessary to safeguard the interests of the company. This means that if there is any doubt, customers have to prove themselves to the powers that be—and this can be very demeaning to people who perceive themselves to be good honest citizens (as most of us are) and therefore beyond suspicion.

GIVING THE BENEFIT OF THE DOUBT

❖ When the customer complains that the food she has been served is cold, don't argue. Don't even raise an eyebrow. Trust that it is cold.

❖ When the customer complains that he has been waiting for more than 20 minutes you might assume he is exaggerating (we all do), but do trust that he has been waiting longer than he reasonably expects. Don't argue.

❖ When the customer phones to inform you that she has not received the item she ordered three weeks ago, don't counter by stating that it was posted two weeks ago and the situation is therefore not your fault. Solve the problem rather than explaining it away.

❖ When a group of teenagers who look no more than 14 years old attempt to enter a club for adults, do not give them the benefit of the doubt. Ask for evidence of their age.

❖ When a customer claims a special discount but states that she has lost her discount card, trust your own judgment of her demeanor, her attitude, and her approach. If you still have a doubt about her integrity, apply the benefit of the doubt and give her the discount anyway.

When you give a customer the benefit of the doubt you will create a buzz. Conversely, the buzz will quickly erode as soon as you begin to doubt your customers and show it.

BUZZ PRACTICE 19
During your regular half-hour team meeting, discuss your customers (internal and external) and the doubts you have about them, and agree how these can be addressed.

BUZZ QUOTE
For buzzing world-class customer relationships, trust and toleration are of the essence. Doubt is the antithesis of trust, and it works both ways.

20 BE GENEROUS WITH CUSTOMERS

Find a way of showing your generosity to the next customer you meet.

In 2003 Happy Computers won the *Management Today* award for providing the best customer service in the UK. An intrinsic part of its philosophy is to be generous with customers. Generosity is a key principle for Henry Stewart, chief executive, Cathy Callus, managing director, and the whole team.

It is called the 110% rule. For every 100% you take from others, give 110% back. That's only reasonable. The world would be a better place if we all practiced this rule—and customer service would be consistently outstanding across the globe.

What will you give your customers today?

We are born to be selfish and we have to struggle to be selfless. In an increasingly competitive world it can be everyone for themselves. Only the fittest survive. Given a chance, many will profiteer at the expense of others, exploiting them for a quick buck.

Instead, perform little acts of generosity for your customers. Every day. Unless your own bosses are generous themselves, don't ask permission—too many managers will be negative and stick to the rules, pleading cost-cutting rationales. They will even forbid you from giving a candy to a customer.

Just do it—be generous. Don't do it with other people's money—because that's not being generous—but do it with your own.

This means being generous with your own time, with your own thoughts, and, if you have any left, with your own money too. If you buy a customer a little gift (it has to be little to avoid accusations of bribery and corruption), then buy it out of your own money.

If your company is sensible enough to budget for such gifts, then treat that budget as if it were your own money. Then you will spend the company's money wisely.

GENEROSITY

✪ If portion controls dictate one scoop of ice cream with apple tart, give an extra large scoop if you think the customer would appreciate it.

✪ If your productivity target is 12 calls an hour, break the rules if need be and give ten minutes to a customer who warrants it.

✪ Buy the customer a complimentary cappuccino.

✪ Keep a bag of mints under the counter to offer customers and ensure that you get through a bag a day (but don't eat them all yourself).

✪ When a customer asks for a couple of samples for the kids, give them eight (in case they plan to have more children).

✪ When entertaining businesspeople for lunch, always be the first to offer to pay the bill.

✪ Don't grieve when people take advantage of you. You will have learnt a lesson in generosity.

✪ Never hesitate to give people something—preferably before they ask for it.

✪ When a customer asks for a discount if she buys three instead of one, give it.

✪ Give money to charity. Give time to charity. Collect money for charity.

There is more motivation and more buzz in giving to a customer than in taking from one. You can't be world-class if you are mean-minded. The companies that are world-class are those that give things away to customers. They are generous and love to give something back—and the same applies to their people on an individual basis.

BUZZ PRACTICE 20
Put your hand in your pocket and spend something on a customer today. That will create a real buzz.

BUZZ QUOTE
Generosity is all about giving something from our heart. When we are generous we give a little of ourselves away.

THE THEATER OF BUZZ

The word "performance" has two related meanings. There is the business definition relating to how well a person or machine is doing. Then there is the theatrical meaning relating to a play or concert attended by an audience.

In practice, what the customer experiences is more like theater. World-class service is a performance of art supported by science and technology.

Buzz is a performance on stage. It is creating a total experience for customers that is both positive and memorable—just like Sir Simon Rattle conducting the Berlin Philharmonic.

21 CREATE A THEATER OF DELIGHT

Delighting customers is all about allowing the light in your heart to shine through to them. Express your delight in seeing each customer.

Today's play in the theater of buzz is about light. Customers should be the light of our working lives. Without customers our world would be dark—the lights in the theater would be off. Without customers our world (and thus our stage) would be empty. We would be unable to perform. That's the world we live in today. Without customers we are nothing.

Customers are wonderful. They are our raison d'être. Life would be so miserable without them. So isn't it strange that it is often the other way round? We make it so miserable for our customers—as if we would rather be without them and the aggravation that we perceive they bring. The buzz removes the misery and creates delight.

World-class customer relations are thus all about light. It should shine out of our hearts, through our faces and voices on to our customers. It should lighten up their days. The buzz is the radiation that comes from this light. It radiates out and warms customers and occasionally excites them. Most definitely it makes them feel good. As Confucius said, "The gold in one's heart is more precious than the gold in one's pocket."

But such delight rarely exists. The other day I strolled through a large shopping mall and dropped into various stores to look around. At no stage was a store assistant delighted to see me. Mostly I was ignored as I browsed the different displays—nobody seemed to know that a potential customer was in the store.

Most people report that call centers are just as bad. There is no delight. The interaction tends to be purely routine and devoid of emotional energy.

Yet surprise, surprise—there are exceptions. One is even called Surprise, a duty restaurant manager at the Holiday Inn Crowne Plaza at Sandton, near Johannesburg in South Africa. He is always delighted to see his customers and to do little extras for them. A broad grin appears on his face as soon as he sees a customer. "Customers make my day," he says. "Where would I be without them? It is a pure delight to serve customers and pure agony not to have any."

The following are ten little things you can do to create a theater of delight:

✔ Show your delight when a customer approaches.
✔ Show your delight when writing a letter to a customer.
✔ Show your delight when a customer brings you a problem.
✔ Show your delight when a customer calls you on the phone.
✔ Show your delight in responding to an email from a customer.
✔ Show your delight in doing anything a customer requests of you, within reason.
✔ Show your delight in taking an initiative for a customer (like obtaining a telephone number).
✔ Show your delight in listening to a customer's story.
✔ Show your delight when a customer is delighted.
✔ Show your delight when a customer returns to your organization.

> **How did you delight a customer today?**

Delight is one of the personal choices we make in formulating our essential attitudes of mind. Our behaviors reflect these choices. An attitude of delight is transmitted into the look on our faces, which light up when we see a customer and have an opportunity to please them.

BUZZ PRACTICE 21
Discover the light inside your heart. Then lighten up and delight a customer with the look on your face.

BUZZ QUOTE
Delight is an attitude that we can all choose for ourselves.

21

22 WARM UP YOUR WELCOME

Ensure that each customer is given a warm and friendly welcome.

When first on stage there should be a look of delight on your face at seeing a customer. Secondly comes the warm welcome. The essence of that warmth is the genuine positive feeling you have for the approaching customer and the energy that flows from your heart toward them.

Some customers argue that they prefer not to have a warm welcome, that they would like to be left alone and not be set upon by some greeter with a gushing welcome.

This presents a quandary that you might care to discuss with your colleagues: "Is it important to welcome customers or not? In other words, should we leave them to get on with what they want to do until such time as they approach us for help?"

There is no simple answer, for the simple reason that in the theater of buzz the art of welcoming a customer requires a range of subtle and complex skills. An over-the-top, programmed, artificial welcome can potentially alienate a customer as much as no welcome at all.

The welcome extended should vary according to the circumstances and so front-line people need to develop their skills in choosing the best type of welcome for any particular customer. However, the key principle is that there must be a welcome and it must be genuine and warm.

What needs to be discussed, refined, and varied as appropriate is the style of welcome. It is critical that you differentiate between a genuine warm welcome and a push for purchase. If a customer senses that you are using the welcome to sell something, inevitably there will be a risk of alienation—unless the customer is intent on buying what you have on offer.

The following are various little things that might comprise the style of your welcome:

- ✪ a passionate hug
- ✪ a kindly greeting
- ✪ a rapturous smile
- ✪ a gentle handshake
- ✪ a friendly acknowledgment
- ✪ an encouraging move toward the customer

Every front-line employee has their stage (or territory), whether it be the tables they look after in a restaurant, the counter at the bank, the sales till in the store, or the desk in the showroom. As soon as a customer comes within the vicinity of that patch, a warm welcome is warranted. The welcome should be irrespective of whether the customer is just looking around, seeking information and advice, or keen to buy something.

The overall purpose of a welcome is to make the customer feel wanted and not neglected. There comes a time when most customers require attention and this is more easily provided if a welcome has been extended in the first instance.

The warm welcome initiates the buzz by establishing the relationship and making it conducive to the next step. This might be answering a query, providing advice, taking an order, or completing a transaction. In other words, the welcome paves the way for customer service that buzzes. The warmer the welcome, the warmer the potential relationship will be—and the better the experience will be for the customer. In the absence of a warm welcome the interaction with a customer (the query, the advice, the order, or the transaction) has to take place from a cold start. A welcome offers a warm start—that's the buzz.

BUZZ PRACTICE 22
With your colleagues, role play different styles of welcome until you perfect the art. Then practice it on each and every customer.

BUZZ QUOTE
The welcome you extend to a customer must vary according to the circumstances.

WORK YOUR EYES

Put your eyes to work in engaging customers.

Eyes are a vital conduit through which you reveal to a customer your soul, heart, and mind. When it comes to face-to-face contact with a customer, the eyes provide the important first connection. There is no avoiding the eyes if world-class service is to be provided. Avoidance means one thing only—that you want to avoid the customer, that you don't want to deal with him or listen to her. It reveals that you have other things on your mind and that the customer in front of you is the least of your priorities.

When you look away from an approaching customer or don't even see them, there is only one conclusion: You would prefer that the customer were not there. Conversely, when customers avert their gaze it means that they require no attention from you at that point—they want to be left alone. By making a connection with your eyes you assign each customer a degree of importance. You reveal that the focus of your attention is the person who has come to be served by you.

However, it is not good enough simply to make eye contact. Each customer will see into your eyes and interpret your intentions. They will see your soul through your eyes and determine whether you are genuine or false, whether you are sincere or shifty, whether you are

 really delighted to see them or just putting on an act because someone in training instructed you to smile at customers.

Your eyes tell a customer as much as your words can. Your eyes will reveal whether or not you are hooked on what a customer is saying and equally whether you really mean what you are saying.

Through your eyes you can produce a glance, a stare, a smile, an inquisitive look, a knowing wink, a gesture of appreciation, a flicker of delight, a sparkle of surprise, a gleam of heart-felt happiness, and a wide variety of other microbehaviors, each of which will have a positive, negative, or neutral impact on customers.

It is worth listing some of the idiomatic expressions in the English language to demonstrate the importance of eyes in relationships:

See eye to eye	An eye-opener	Eye-catching
Eye someone up	Close your eyes to	An eye for an eye
Give someone the eye	Have an eye for	Keep an eye out for
Eyes in the back of your head	Keep your eyes open	Open someone's eyes
Up to the eyes in	A roving eye	Keep an eye on
(I am) all eyes	Make eyes at	An eye for the ladies
An eye for a bargain	Eye witness	Eye-popping
A twinkle in the eye	An eyeful	Turn a blind eye
One in the eye for	The eye of a storm	

All these reflect nuances in the way we use our eyes to connect with customers and provide subtle indicators of our intention in a relationship. Finessing the movement, focus, and expression of our eyes is thus something crucial we need to do in creating a buzz. The essential and underlying principle is that the resulting look must truly reflect our souls and what is in our hearts. Any other reading will be false.

Many people are totally unaware of what is happening with their eyes and what they reveal to people at any given moment. Those who excel at "working their eyes" are those who excel at service and in creating a buzz.

BUZZ PRACTICE 23
Conduct an eye test with those of your colleagues you really trust. Invite them to describe your eyes and then reciprocate. Then practice working your eyes to reflect the positive spirit you have inside you.

BUZZ QUOTE
In any face-to-face relationship with a customer the start point is always the eyes.

WORK YOUR VOICE

Give voice to your positive feelings for customers.

The voice is multifaceted and with the exception of opera singers, stage actors, and public speakers, it is much ignored as an instrument for connecting with customers. Most of us rely on our "default" voice, without thinking whether there are better options in the way we use our voice to express ourselves to customers. This default voice is a product of our upbringing and one to which most people pay little attention. We are unaware of how we sound and the impact this has on others. Tone, pace, clarity, intensity, and intent as well as vocabulary and idiom are vital factors in determining the way we express ourselves. In other words, to tune in to customers we have to fine-tune our voices.

There is a vast variety of options in working your voice and the correct choice will greatly enhance your prospects of influencing and delighting your customers. Thus the skill of persuasion is not simply a matter of the words selected but of the way those words are voiced. Articulation is one of the arts of customer service that requires the exercise of vocal nuance for maximum impact. It is the little things that individuals do with their voices that can make a big difference in communicating with customers.

Modulation of the voice requires energy and a high degree of consciousness of how you sound to other people. In working your voice you need to be sensitive to the effect of your words on the other person. You need to ask yourselves questions such as: "Have I really connected with the customer? Is she listening or just hearing? Can I adjust my voice to secure a more effective engagement with her?"

Each customer is different and the key skill in communicating is to select expressions that maximize the probability of commanding their attention and engaging them. Thus if the customer is not fluent in

English you should speak at a slower pace with full attention given to clear articulation. The same applies if the customer is a senior citizen who is a little hard of hearing.

For example, there are a wide variety of ways of engaging a customer who is browsing:

FACTORS	INAPPROPRIATE CHOICE	APPROPRIATE CHOICE
Choice of words	"Good morning madam, can I help you?"	"Forgive me for intruding, but just to let you know I'm over there if you need some help"
Tone	Cold/mechanistic/matter-of-fact	Warm/genuine/motivated
Pace	Too fast	Appropriately paced
Clarity	Muffled	Clear articulation
Intensity	Too soft	Not too loud, not too soft
Intent	Routine task, go through motions	Sincere effort to help

Emotional tone is significant here. The amount of feeling pumped into any one word or short phrase will register with the customer, who will interpret your sincerity or disinterest accordingly. As such the voice can almost sing with melody as opposed to sounding flat. Some people's voices drone while others allow their happiness to infiltrate every sound. Equally, some people have voices that are abrupt or clipped and thus alienate, while others have soft, warm, rounded voices that reassure and attract.

Become conscious of how your voice currently sounds and all the little things that can be done to modulate and enhance it.

BUZZ PRACTICE 24
Listen carefully to other people's voices and gauge the impact they have on you.
Now record your own voice and try to gauge the impact this has on others. Encourage your colleagues to be honest with you: does your voice sound positive?

BUZZ QUOTE
A positive heart will invariably lead to a positive voice.

24

25 TOUCH YOUR CUSTOMERS

The ultimate connection in customer relations is when customers are touched by you. Touch your customers' hearts.

To create a buzz you need to touch your customers, in every sense of the word. This is pure theater. You need to move them emotionally in such a positive way that they want to repeat the experience. They will thus be touched by what you do for them and furthermore will want to get in touch with you again. This is the ultimate customer connection.

However, in this chapter the focus will be on the most controversial aspect of touching customers—physically touching them. In deference to political correctness, sexual equality, and abhorrence of abuse and molestation, it is quite natural that many people shy away from what used to come quite naturally to them, making physical contact. Yet when this is done effectively it can add immense value in cementing a relationship. It is almost like "pressing the buzzer."

There can be no absolute rule on when to touch a customer physically and when not to. The exercise of sound judgment and innocent intent are essential. You might argue that in many instances it would be highly inappropriate and furthermore high risk. Yet does this mean you should not offer to shake the hand of most customers? Shaking hands is an initial touch and the initiative must come from you. By offering your hand you offer a connection that initiates a relationship with a new customer or consolidates an existing one.

There are many different ways of shaking hands, from a brief shake to a firm grasp or a two-handed shake by which a customer's right hand is clasped and shaken while your left hand takes his or her elbow and reinforces the shake. This can prove to be a very powerful welcoming touch—or a rather pleasing farewell touch.

There are other physical touches that can have a positive impact on customers. While there are obvious forbidden zones, there are two safe zones that are acceptable and risk little misinterpretation (assuming the touch is of exquisitely high moral intent): the shoulder and the elbow.

Tapping someone lightly on the shoulder to reassure can strike an important emotional chord. Similarly, guiding a customer by the elbow can indicate genuine personal support.

In addition to the safe zones, there are some of intermediate risk where a touch can be highly appropriate or equally inappropriate. The first is touching a customer's hand. Holding an old lady's hand when she is in distress can strike a reassuring emotional chord. The second example is putting your arm around a customer's shoulder. When appropriate this can indicate genuine friendship as you walk along and perhaps crack a joke.

Get in touch with your customers

One high-risk touch that causes much confusion is kissing a customer on the cheek. Should you do it at all? Should you do it once, twice, or three times? The general rule is to avoid doing so unless you know the customer very well and wish to greet him or her like a real friend. In this case, greeting customers with a kiss on the cheek is acceptable if not essential.

Culture inevitably comes into the arena of touching and the recommendations above have to be tempered by the local customs and traditions of your country. This chapter has been written mainly with westerners in mind. Touching is also discussed in *The Biz*.

BUZZ PRACTICE 25
These behaviors can be so controversial and risky that it is worth having a debate about them with your colleagues. Encourage them to read this section and pose the question: "Is it desirable to touch customers physically and if so in what circumstances?" Then perhaps you should practice it among yourselves.

BUZZ QUOTE
Get in touch with your customers. Touch their hearts. Touch them.

25

CHOOSE YOUR SMILE

Someone with a permanent smile is no more friendly than someone who never smiles. Consider your smile and choose the genuine version.

One of the clichés in the early debates about customer service was the "smile factor." In so-called charm schools it was felt that the production of a smile was sufficient to deliver excellent customer service. It seemed that smiling was the answer to all customer service problems—and not enough people had the answer.

The answer in fact lies not in the smile, but in the type of smile chosen. There are many different types.

TYPES OF SMILE
Genuine smile
Warm smile
Wry smile
False smile
Mocking smile
Knowing smile

Smiling does not come easily to many people. Any study of the human face will reveal that most people have a default look, just like their default voice. This is the expression (or lack of expression) to which people revert when nothing is happening, when they are standing on trains, waiting in queues, sitting on benches, or walking unaccompanied along the street. When they are alone people rarely smile—and if they did we might think them a little strange.

Smiling occurs mainly when we are with other people. It can come naturally because we are pleased to see them or because we are amused by something they have said or done. It can be an automatic response (because we intuitively smile at everything) or it can be chosen.

The smile is a behavioral instrument that puts others at their ease and makes them feel good. When overdone there is a risk that people become suspicious: "How can this person be smiling all the time? Are they never serious? Are they all surface and no depth? Do they live off their charm?"

Thus too much smiling can be as bad for a relationship with a customer as no smiling at all. Too much smiling creates concerns that you are false, not genuine, and are acting out a role—merely pouring behavioral honey onto each and every interaction with a customer.

Conversely, if you don't smile customers may feel that you don't like them and are not interested in developing a commercial relationship with them.

How do you choose to smile?

Smiling is a choice that should genuinely reflect happiness. If you don't feel pleasure at seeing another person, you should not smile.

One little thing you can do, therefore, is not to allow your face to revert to its default position when you are with other people. By focusing your attention on customers you can train yourself to be conscious of the expression on your face and thus choose the appropriate moment to smile, perhaps when welcoming the customer, perhaps when they have something interesting to say, perhaps when they are pleased with what is going on.

The key is to make your smile special, so that it has maximum impact in building and reinforcing the relationship with a customer. When you choose to feel special about a customer who is walking through the door, that is the time to give that particular customer a special smile.

BUZZ PRACTICE 26
Become "smile conscious." Practice smiling on chosen occasions and in doing so become aware of the type of smile that you choose.

BUZZ QUOTE
Smiling at customers will make you happy.

26

27 HAVE A LAUGH WITH YOUR CUSTOMERS

Crack a joke and have fun with a customer today.

Richard Reed, one of the founders of Innocent Drinks (UK), has installed a "banana phone" for his customers to ring any time. His products, which include yoghurt-based smoothies, are delivered in a "cowavan," a delivery van that looks like a cow.

Not everyone has the same sense of humor. If we did there would be a formula for it and we would all laugh at the same time. But we don't, so what is funny for one person is no joke for another. Some people always see the serious side and never recognize the pun. They take things literally when they are really said in jest. When you say "This is so awful I am going to cry all the way home," they really do expect you to cry.

Laughing and joking can therefore be high risk. Because we don't want to offend customers, we don't risk the joke. It is no fun when work is like this. The establishment risks becoming humorless and as gray and boring as any place where no risks are taken and no buzz is created. Amusement is an important element of the theater of buzz.

The secret is never to make fun at the customer's (or other people's) expense. Nobody finds it funny to be mocked, for example pointing to a customer's striped shirt and commenting, "I like your new pyjamas." This is not funny, at least to the poor man wearing the shirt. However, if you ask a customer "Do you like my new pyjamas?" while pointing to your own striped shirt, you have to take the risk that the customer understands what you are saying—or, to express it more exactly, understands what you are not saying.

Humor should only be personal if you yourself are the butt of the joke. It is preferable to be impersonal and make jokes like "We've never had a complaint about this laptop—that's because we've never sold one before" or "This brand of adhesive is excellent, most customers stick to it all the time."

Most interactions with customers present some opportunity for humor, no matter how mild—and sometimes the milder the humor the more amusing and acceptable it is. Amusement and humor stimulate the flow of serotonin in the body and this makes customers feel good. It puts people at their ease, the humor smoothing the way for a transaction and reducing any stress involved in a purchase.

BUZZ BOOK OF LAUGHTER

Create your own buzz book of jokes and laughter. Then test one or two on customers.

When they laugh or smile you will know you are on to a winner.

The key to humor is the unexpected, for example commenting to a customer coming in from the rain, "What beautiful weather we are having today!" There are creative opportunities all the time for amusing statements, such as "When you pay here we always guarantee a free paper receipt," or "These products last a lifetime, our customers are always coming back for them."

It takes very little to amuse a customer. All that is required is imagination and a little risk taking. It's far better to get a customer to smile at some humorous comment than to say nothing. The joke might also spark a response from a customer that amuses you and even makes your day. The spiraling escalation of funny comments can create the buzz as people vie with each other to say something even funnier.

As the saying goes, "The customer always has the last laugh."

BUZZ PRACTICE 27
Challenge yourself to crack a joke with a customer today. It only a takes a little thing to make a customer smile.

BUZZ QUOTE
Few areas of life are so serious that you can't find something amusing in what is happening.

28 CELEBRATE WITH YOUR CUSTOMERS

Look out for and seize opportunities to celebrate with your customers. Celebrate something today.

Although few of us do it, we should celebrate being alive, celebrate being a human as opposed to a frog, and simply celebrate every day that we can wake up, enjoy our families, earn a few cents at work, eat the

occasional burger, and meet some wonderful people. Yet most of us take this for granted and some even complain when things don't live up to our inflated expectations.

Customers have a lot to celebrate too. That is what often takes them shopping, banking, traveling, and generally out and about. To create a fantastic buzz one of the tricks is to discover things you can celebrate with customers.

Stephanie Wing, a former guest relations officer at the Veranda Hotel in Grand Baie, Mauritius, asked for passports at check-in. She made a careful note of each customer's birthday and then sent them a celebratory ecard. If the birthday occurred during the guest's stay, she arranged a little celebration at dinner, perhaps a special cake.

Some front-line staff just celebrate having customers. Herman Aquino is head waiter at the Tong Yang Restaurant in Malate, Philippines and most of his customers are local, from the Ermita district of Manila. He celebrates their wedding anniversaries and birthdays with cakes and music from mariachis. However, when the restaurant has visitors from abroad he will also celebrate this, clapping his hands, announcing to the locals that they are privileged to have foreign customers, then serenading the customers with music before presenting them with a special cake adorned with a lighted candle.

66

Celebration is of course a matter of judgment and there is always a risk of going over the top. However, if the celebration is skillfully judged nine times out of ten the customer will appreciate it. The key is to make the celebration personal as opposed to routine. A company should avoid programming celebrations by automatically sending preprinted birthday cards to customers. The personal touch is essential if the celebration is to mean anything and that means having people in your company who have built up relationships with individual customers and who look out for opportunities to celebrate.

Here are some further examples of little things you can do to celebrate:

- Send a personalized birthday card to a customer (when you have spotted the date from their personal details).
- Send a card to celebrate an anniversary (when you have encountered a customer buying an anniversary present).
- Present a small gift when a regular customer has a baby.
- Give a customer a celebratory shake of the hand when she informs you that she has just passed her examinations, perhaps followed up with a "well done" card.
- When you read about a customer's achievements in a local newspaper (at sport, to do with charity, getting promoted, winning a prize), ring that customer up to congratulate him.
- Give a customer a small memento on the tenth anniversary of when she first did business with you.
- If you note that a customer is about to retire, write a personal letter to celebrate his past achievements and future successes.
- Celebrate the news of a customer's engagement with a glass of champagne.

BUZZ PRACTICE 28

Set yourself and your colleagues a challenge: "This week we will find one special event to celebrate with customers." If you set your minds on this you will discover something.

BUZZ POINT
Every time a customer makes a major purchase is a cause for celebration.

28

29 TURN YOUR CUSTOMERS INTO CELEBRITIES

You don't need to be Wayne Rooney to be a star, you just need to be a customer under the influence of the buzz. Make a celebrity of at least one customer today.

Customers are the star performers of the business world. They score the goals for you, get your team to number one in the service league, and should be featured as icons of wise choice. You are the supporters who help get them there, who turn your customers into celebrities because of their rare talents (aiming for the best and getting the best from you).

By giving your customers the VIP treatment you are putting into practice one of the earliest rules of customer service: "Customers are very important people." It is worth stating, because in so many establishments this rule is never applied. Customers are not made to feel important at all, in fact they are given less importance than the task in hand, whether it be sticking price tickets on stock, creating displays, operating the till, or processing a transaction. In these situations customers do not exist and they feel it: they might as well be elsewhere. They are definitely not star attractions.

Turning your customers into celebrities becomes a self-fulfilling prophecy. When you make someone feel like a star, sooner or later they will start acting like one. The secret is to make the customer feel not merely an important person but a very important person, someone who is a celebrity in your book. When customers walk through the door your challenge is to make them feel like the most important person in the world. In fact, when they walk through the door everything should stop—as it does for someone famous.

Customers are celebrities who attract everyone's eyes, whom people rush to be near, with whom front-liners want to have a few words. Customers are so precious that a moment of time spent with them will linger long in the memory— their glorious purchases transformed into your personal glory at work.

You're a star!

At a branch of the Superquinn supermarket group in Ireland, employees stick badges on children as they enter the store. They are treated like stars.

While you can put customers on the front page of the company newsletter or get them to sponsor an advertisement, that is not the only route to celebrity. The star performers are those whom people talk about, tell stories about—and then, occasionally, they are the people who receive a great deal of media attention and who crop up in the newspapers and elsewhere.

Celebrities have fans—and if you are not a fan of your customers then you will never create a buzz.

When you treat customers like celebrities everyone gets excited, everyone cheers, and the red carpet is laid out across your patch. Everyone is on parade for a customer and on the rare occasions when something goes wrong (even David Beckham has poor matches) people feel disappointed.

Celebrities are well known within the wide boundaries of their profession. Thus it is important that individual customers become well known within the wide boundaries of a company's custom.

BUZZ PRACTICE 29
One little thing you can do today is treat at least one customer like a celebrity. Just tell her she is a star and see how she reacts!

BUZZ POINT
Five-star service requires you to treat your customers like stars.

29

30 DECORATE YOUR PERSONAL SPACE

Express yourself through decoration. Change your decorations today.

Institutions are the worst kind of place, because there is an absence of decoration. The walls are featureless, the corridors are dull, and the rooms are gray. The noticeboards are full of small-print regulations and the whole environment reflects a dreariness of repetitive bureaucracy undertaken by expressionless people bored out of their wits. Monotony and mind-numbing tedium are the order of the day. Balzac, Kafka, and William Whyte wrote about these places and they still exist. Effectively, people have lost their souls to the restraints of higher powers. The lackluster approach is reflected on to customers who, now accustomed to the stimulus of modern life, become alienated by the absence of energy in such dark, intimidating places.

LITTLE DECORATIVE TOUCHES

Yellow balloons
Primary school art
Quotes from favorite authors
Pink and purple streamers
Prints of peaceful places
Visitors' book
Celebration chocolates
Posters of pop or movie stars
Postcards from exotic places
Vases of daffodils
Gold-plated pens
Photos of family
Teddy bears

Enlightened organizations delight their customers by sparking positive energy. The buzz occurs when people's souls light up and are expressed through imagination and creative endeavor. In the theater of buzz the stage for enlightenment and delight is your personal space (or your territory or patch or whatever you like to call it). A key aspect of this is how you decorate your surroundings.

Your personality, and thus your heart and soul, is reflected in the way you do this. It reveals part of you by demonstrating how colorful, creative, and fascinating you can be as opposed to being untidy, drab, or boring. In other words, walls talk. You can tell the nature of an organization from its internal walls and surroundings and how they are used by the people working within them.

People who buzz decorate their walls, screens, and their personal space with balloons, streamers, photographs, and quotes of the day. On the desk you will find complimentary candies, dolls, ornaments, or giveaways that front-line people really want to give away. What you find is a personal expression of self as individuals extend themselves to the outer boundaries of their personal space. The environment becomes a projection of individual and team spirit and effectively the staging and lighting for the performance enjoyed by customers. Nikki, a receptionist at Saxon Weald Housing in Horsham, UK, adorns her counter with lollipops for visiting children.

There can be no rule, no system, no standard for such decoration. Tedium sets in when the building services department, forever cost conscious, declares a policy that posters must not be stuck on walls (for fear of damaging the surface) and decorations are not to be suspended from the ceiling.

You should not be told what you can do to decorate your personal stage and thus make it come alive in performing for your customers. One team I came across put a bucket in the middle of their open-plan office and team members were encouraged to donate money to charity on the weekly mufti (casual dress) day for the privilege of wearing jeans and T-shirts to work. That created a buzz, not only for the team and visitors to the office but also for the charity that benefited.

BUZZ PRACTICE 30
Purge your desk, your office, and all your workspace of clutter. Then redecorate it so that it will be immensely appealing to all your customers and visitors.

BUZZ QUOTE
Create, decorate, and stimulate. That's the buzz.

30

THE HEART OF BUZZ

The buzz emanates from the positive emotional energies that are sparked in the hearts and souls of employees who love to produce memorable experiences for customers.

Emotional intelligence, emotional competence, and added emotional value all have vital parts to play. These relate to people's desires and intrinsic motivations to switch customers on and make them feel good. The motivational drive for the buzz is emotional, not intellectual.

When there is a buzz customers feel it. It is not a thought process by which customers analyze their experience, tick boxes on a survey form, and conclude that their experience was buzzing. They sense the buzz. They experience it.

31 PUT TIME INTO THE RELATIONSHIP

Relationships need to be developed and reinforced by doing additional little things for customers.

Progressive companies start the buzz at the top. Their chief executives want to build and develop relationships with customers as well as employees. It is one of their top priorities.

For example Alan Jones, the previous group managing director of TNT Express at Atherstone in the UK, had a simple policy. Customers would be able to speak to (and relate to) any person in the company they chose. Thus if a customer wanted to speak to Alan Jones he would personally take the call. There was no telephone screening by the dreaded gatekeepers you find in other companies. This policy effectively

removed any barriers to developing the essential relationships between customers and company.

Dan Watkins, managing director of Birmingham Midshires Bank in Wolverhampton, UK, and his team have the same approach. They are prepared to invest time in listening to customers. In fact, they are so keen to speak to customers that they put their own business and home telephone numbers on the bank's website.

Andrew Messenger, chief executive of the West Bromwich building society, also reflects this attitude: "It's all about 'people, people, people.' That is our secret."

These senior executives lead by example, demonstrating that they are prepared to invest time, effort, and energy in developing relationships with customers and employees alike.

Doing so requires no more than devoting a little extra time to people and where possible doing something for them. It might be as simple as being prepared to listen to them or following up on some issue that they raised recently.

All relationships become tired and jaded. The energy drains out as we fall into routine and habit. Thus to sustain and develop the relationship we need time and a fresh stimulus applied on a periodic basis.

Invest 15 minutes of your time today developing relationships with your customers

"We have customers who will come to one of our branches in the morning to withdraw £10 and then return in the afternoon to deposit the same £10," says Andrew Messenger. "Our customers in these branches get a buzz out of the relationship they have with our staff."

The opportunities for developing relationships are endless. They can come from learning a little more about a customer, or from giving a customer an occasional call, or simply from dropping everything to deal with a customer's problem. Sometimes a brief chat is all that is needed. The overall outcome is that each customer feels valued because you are putting your valuable time and energy into the relationship. It only means a minute here and an action there, but each of these timely efforts feeds, nourishes, and sustains the relationship.

BUZZ PRACTICE 31
Take one action every day that is devoted to developing a relationship with an existing customer. It might be sending a short email containing something interesting, or spending an extra few minutes chatting with a customer about the football match the previous evening.

BUZZ QUOTE
The more you invest in developing relationships with customers the more successful you will become.

32 EMPATHIZE

Adopt a high degree of sensitivity toward your customers' emotions and develop your understanding of them.

Forget your own feelings—much more important are your customers' feelings. Emotional intelligence is all about detecting and understanding how other people feel and responding in a sensitive and intelligent way.

People who have superb relationship skills are well able to detect the nuances of emotions expressed by other people. They can pick up an angry look on someone's face or detect that this person is distressed or that one excited.

A wide range of emotions are important in customer relationships. Here are just a few:

Enjoyment—amusement, delight, happiness, joy, pride, relief, thrill.
Love—caring, fondness, generosity, protection.
Acceptance—friendliness, harmony, kindness, trust, warmth.
Surprise—amazement, astonishment, dismay, shock, wonder.
Sadness—despair, loneliness, sorrow, unhappiness.
Shame—embarrassment, guilt, regret, remorse.
Negativity—coldness, distance, distrust, rejection.
Disgust—disdain, distaste, scorn, slight.
Anger—animosity, annoyance, exasperation, fury, indignation, outrage.
Fear—alarm, anxiety, apprehension, concern, insecurity, horror, trouble.

One of the little things you can do every day is to extend your emotional antennae toward each customer and try to detect how they are feeling. In the first instance you can tell whether they are demonstrating positive or negative emotions—or no emotions at all. Then as your skills in empathy develop you will be able to detect one or more of the emotions listed above. This will enable you to respond much more effectively.

The skill in empathy is to demonstrate that you understand and accept (as opposed to reject) the customer's emotions. It is no good saying to a customer, "You have no reason to be angry with us because it is not our fault the product is damaged and you have had to bring it back." It is far better to say, "I would be angry too if this product had let me down in the way it has for you. I can well appreciate the inconvenience you have suffered by bringing it all the way back."

Similarly, if a customer is excited because she is about to go on vacation to Florida, a skilled front-line employee will be able to share in that excitement too.

The key is to accept customers for what they are. If they are full of rage then you have to accept this, try to understand the rage, and help them convert this negative emotion into a positive one—by doing something positive for them.

What is your customer feeling now?

Another example is when a customer feels guilty because this is the third time he has troubled you with the same problem. An unskilled employee can make the customer feel bad with a simple "tut-tut" or a look of scorn or annoyance. The customer's self-esteem suffers because he believes that the employee thinks he is an idiot. A skilled employee will empathize and provide some positive emotional reassurance that it is no trouble, in fact it is a pleasure.

Our relationships are built or damaged by such subtle interchanges of emotional signals. Empathy is the critical component here for success.

Emotions are infectious and this can be good or bad. You should never allow a customer's negative emotion (such as irritation) to infect you by making you irritated too. But there is no harm in allowing a customer's positive emotion to influence your feelings. In fact, it works both ways. As explained in Chapter 21, if you are delighted to see a customer then the probability is that the customer will be delighted to see you. That is empathy working in its most powerful way.

BUZZ PRACTICE 32
With one of your colleagues, refer to the list of emotions and tick off those your customers are displaying today. What should be your response?

BUZZ QUOTE
The most important quality of emotional intelligence is empathy.

32

33 GO OUT OF YOUR WAY TO HELP

If you don't help your customers, who will? Initiate that help at every opportunity.

Eileen Smithers walked into a department store and started browsing in the stationery section. She came across a diary she liked, but could not find a price on it anywhere. Nearby was an assistant who had not noticed her. The assistant was working with her eyes down, looking at some documentation. Eileen approached her and asked, "Could you tell me the price of this diary please?" The assistant looked displeased at being interrupted. "There is a scanner over there," she snorted, pointing toward a pillar. Eileen could not see the price scanner and furthermore was unsure how to operate it. She put the diary down and left.

Companies that buzz excel in providing help. Customers know exactly who to turn to when they run into difficulties. Not only does the company have a system in place that facilitates help, it also has people who are predisposed to help. In fact they relish the prospect of doing little things for customers—putting themselves out if necessary in terms of time and effort to ensure that a customer's inconvenience is minimized and any problem resolved.

This might be as simple as offering to carry a customer's shopping to the car, or volunteering to complete a complicated registration form on his or her behalf. It might be calling a supplier to obtain additional information about the equipment rather than insisting that the customer call after returning home.

In buzzing organizations employees go looking for opportunities to help. They will discover customers looking lost on the concourse and volunteer to take them wherever they wish, they will encounter customers who are frustrated in finding the right person to talk to and put them in contact with that person, they will search for an item a customer cannot find in stock, they will investigate a delay and get back to the customer, they will take time out to explain to a customer something he or she does not understand.

Helping people is one of the greatest pleasures in life. The altruism it reflects is at the core of teams that buzz.

Too often companies seem distant and unwilling to help. This happens when you ring certain financial institutions and insurance companies with remote call centers. Every time you manage to get through to a human being it is a different person and you have to repeat your cry for help and elaborate on the history and circumstances. Even then, the call center agents can seem reluctant to help if the problem is something out of the ordinary.

Helping a customer is a top priority and requires you to put aside other lower-priority tasks to bring about a resolution to the customer's problem.

HELP!
"My flight has been canceled."
"I've tried 20 times to call the number and there's no response."
"You've sent me a threatening letter when I've already paid."
"I was told yesterday that someone would call back. Nobody has."
"I waited in all morning and the engineer didn't turn up."
"I was told last week that the letter was in the post. I still haven't received it."

BUZZ PRACTICE 33
Become a "customer helper." Be the person the customer turns to when help is needed. Never refer the customer to other people but instead ensure that you are the first to help.

BUZZ QUOTE
When in customers are in need of help you should be there for them.

33

34 TAKE THE LEAD

You don't have to wait for the official leader to take the lead. Take the lead now—that's at the heart of the buzz!

At the heart of the buzz is every individual's desire to take the lead in creating the most positive experience possible for customers. This means that everyone is effectively an unofficial leader.

In a soccer team the lead is not always taken by the captain. It can be taken by a defender who scores a goal or by a forward who decides to back up the defense. In an excellent team everyone takes the lead by positioning themselves for the maximum benefit of the team.

Taking the lead requires a whole series of individual decisions on behalf of a customer without reference to the boss. That's the buzz. These decisions can be big or small—for example whether or not to order and pay for a taxi home for a customer who suddenly falls ill.

Whoever spots the customer first should take the lead in helping that customer. Don't ask your boss. Ask yourself: "Should I or shouldn't I?" Then take the lead in making your own decision on behalf of the customer.

This is the famous inverted triangle:

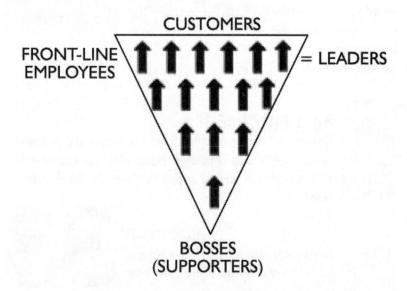

In practice, the inverted triangle means that whoever first encounters a customer's problem should take the lead in resolving that problem. Whoever sees an opportunity to please a customer should take the lead in doing so. Taking the lead at every available opportunity leads to world-class customer service.

When you have a traditional hierarchical organization where the CEO is at the top and customers and employees are at the bottom, a buzz can never be created because everything goes up to the boss. Creating the buzz requires the energy flow in the organization to be reversed. The positive energy should be flowing toward customers, not toward bosses. In fact, it should be flowing away from the bosses. They should not be absorbing energy but dissipating it.

> ## TAKE THE LEAD IN:
>
> ### Spending money on a customer in distress
>
> ### Stepping outside routine to help a customer
>
> ### Initiating contact with a customer who looks lost in another department

In practical terms this requires the much-debated empowering (or enabling) of front-line people to make decisions in favor of customers. It means training everyone at the front line to take the lead in doing whatever is necessary to attract and retain customers. This is a huge challenge for many autocratic organizations that alienate customers (and employees) by insisting that decisions gravitate toward the top.

Thus for the buzz to be created an immense amount of trust is needed. The official leaders have to trust the unofficial ones. The assigned leaders have to support the unassigned people who take the lead.

BUZZ PRACTICE 34

Send the boss away for a few days so that you can have total freedom to take the lead in making decisions. Bring in the buzz and bring back the boss to demonstrate it.

BUZZ POINT
To lead, let the people take the lead.

34

35 STIMULATE TEAM SPIRIT

The buzz can only be created when a team is inspired to work well together.

Inspiration literally means "putting the spirit into" a person or a team. To create an inspirational approach to teamwork, each individual's spirit has to be stimulated. Anybody can do this, not just the boss. When team spirit is stimulated a buzz is created that results in a whole host of little things that people do to please their customers.

The best type of stimulus is a personal challenge, for example challenging everyone to become world-class in every interaction with customers. But it also requires a team challenge, good leadership, and excellent motivation—subjects dealt with at greater length in *The Biz*, the companion book to this one. Here are some examples of behaviors that stimulate team spirit:

- ✪ Denny observes a group of customers suddenly descending on Leah. He gathers together a couple of colleagues and the three of them go over to provide some welcome relief to Leah in helping her serve the customers.

- ✪ Evelyn has a bad experience with an abusive customer. Monette and Jane take her to the back office, give her a cup of tea to settle her down, and provide some moral support.

- ✪ Bernie volunteers to go and fetch a spare part that Nat requires urgently for a customer.

- ✪ Franko starts serenading two customers who are celebrating an anniversary. Joey, Nadine, Mandy, and Malcolm join in and improvise a short song-and-dance routine, to the delight of the two customers and others near them.

- ✪ Emerging from the back office, Vikash sees that a long queue has formed at the counters. He eases the pressure on staff by reassuring the customers that they will be dealt with as quickly as possible, and then arranges for additional counters to be opened.

- ✪ Sonia's mother is taken seriously ill, which means that Sonia has to flex her hours to visit the hospital and also pick up her kids from school, which her mum usually does. The team rallies round and rearranges their rosters to ensure that they can cover for Sonia and customers are not let down.

- ✪ Lance eventually gets his black belt in judo. Shelley, Muriel, Mamed, and Jureen arrange complimentary champagne for customers in celebration. They explain why and it creates a buzz all day.

- ✪ Brenda organizes a "customer of the day" challenge for the whole team. At the end of the day she sits down for five minutes with Russell, Mindi, Nathan, and Karmjit to discuss their experiences with customers and to elect the "customer of the day." Brenda rings up the customer the next day to inform her and to say that a gift voucher is in the post.

- ✪ Sidney brings in a tray of donuts for the team first thing in the morning. He also offers them to early-bird customers.
- ✪ Jay organizes a "red day" for the business. Everyone has to have something red on. Irving sports a red tie while Marc comes to work wearing red lipstick and rouge on his cheeks. Dolly brings a red handbag while Maeve kicks in with red shoes. Customers are encouraged to "spot the red." Michelle continually blushes when customers ask her, "What's red on you?"

Create the spirit of buzz in your team

Teamwork involves continual creativity to stimulate the motivational buzz that customers love. It is a form of magic that appeals to most people and that they sense when they step across the threshold. The intended transaction ceases to be mechanically functional but instead becomes an emotional event of immense attraction to customers. They want to be there because the team is buzzing and they like the experience.

It is all the little things that team members do for each other that add up to make a difference not only for the team itself but for everyone around, including customers. It happens when each team member is switched on. They switch each other on. There is a spark. There is electricity. The undercurrent pulsates with positive energy and this radiates throughout the business and is readily detected by customers. It's almost magic because it's almost unbelievable.

This can happen on an aeroplane, in a restaurant, within a bank, and around a major department store. It can happen in a public service office such as a housing department or even a police station. It can happen in the back office as much as on the front line. When a team wants to buzz it can happen anywhere and anytime.

BUZZ PRACTICE 35
Get the team together and discuss:
❖ What stops the buzz?
❖ What starts the buzz?
Then start it.

BUZZ QUOTE
The more brilliant the team, the bigger the buzz.

THE BUZZ ACADEMY

Teams that buzz are full of fascinating people. For a start, they are fascinated by customers. Buzzing team members have open minds and are always asking questions. They never stop learning and have their own personal academy for doing so. They are inquisitive and want to know more: about customers, about competitors, about the company, about products, and most importantly about how to deliver world-class service consistently.

Inquisitiveness is the precursor to this personal learning academy. Nobody can enhance their know-how, skills, and wisdom unless they devote precious time to digging out new knowledge, developing new skills, and becoming wiser by the day.

Participants in the buzz academy are on a voyage of discovery during which they exercise their skills in listening and observation. They notice things that are different as opposed to seeing the same things all the time. They challenge themselves to push back the boundaries and find a better way.

Overall, in creating a buzz and delivering world-class service they create an academy in their own minds.

36 LEARN ABOUT CUSTOMERS

Learn something new about a customer every day.

Learning comes naturally to people who are inquisitive. By asking simple little questions they dig out new and useful bits of information that they assemble into knowledge that becomes available for application and good practice.

This especially applies to the practice of building relationships with customers and delivering world-class service. The more you learn about your customers, the better you will be able to relate to them and the more answers you will have to help them.

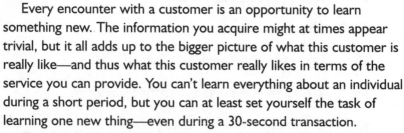

By treating your customers all the same you learn nothing about them. The key is to learn how any one customer is different from all the others and thus to learn how to respond in a special way to that customer's unique requirements. This is at the core of building meaningful relationships with customers.

Every encounter with a customer is an opportunity to learn something new. The information you acquire might at times appear trivial, but it all adds up to the bigger picture of what this customer is really like—and thus what this customer really likes in terms of the service you can provide. You can't learn everything about an individual during a short period, but you can at least set yourself the task of learning one new thing—even during a 30-second transaction.

The people who excel at service and create a buzz are those who seize every precious moment with a customer to increase their information about that person. They go beyond the routine and add a learning dimension to each encounter. They are forever building up their knowledge of customers, about their habits, their business, and their desires, so that when the opportunity arises they are in the best position to help.

Among the things that can be learnt about customers are:

- ❖ What they did last weekend.
- ❖ How their grandchildren are.
- ❖ Who their favorite sports star is.
- ❖ Whether they saw the game last night.
- ❖ Who they think is going to win the election.
- ❖ What they think of this front-page news item.
- ❖ How they got to work on the day of the strike.
- ❖ What they are planning to do for the weekend.
- ❖ When they are going up to town to see the show.
- ❖ How they liked the new product they bought last time.
- ❖ When they are going to start redecorating.
- ❖ Whether they have tried the new Chinese restaurant along the road.
- ❖ Whether they have been on vacation, where they went, and whether they enjoyed it.

By asking this kind of question you can learn a lot about a customer. Over a period of time you build up a picture that presents a frame of reference for future conversation and relationship building. The more you learn about a customer, the more reference points are available for further learning and further relationship building. From this you can detect the customer's needs and are then in the ideal position to help him or her meet these needs.

For example, you might learn that a customer's daughter is about to go to university, so this would be the ideal time to have a chat about opening a bank account. Or you might learn that a customer's best friend is starting a new business and is looking for some help with accountancy.

BUZZ PRACTICE 36
Set yourself a challenge of learning something new about at least one customer each day. Make a note of what you learn. As soon as you become proficient at this, set yourself the even tougher challenge of learning something new about every single customer you encounter each day.

BUZZ QUOTE
Every encounter with a customer presents an opportunity to learn something.

36

37 LISTEN TO CUSTOMERS

If you want customers to listen to your sales pitch, you had better listen to them in the first place. Listen carefully right now to what a customer has to say.

The best way to alienate your customers is not to listen to them. If you do that you will never understand them or learn from them.

We are all experts in talking, but few of us are experts in listening. Most of us like the sound of our own voices more than the sound of others. Visit any public place (such as a shop or a restaurant) and discreetly listen in to what other people are saying. You will find a lot of people talking to others who are not listening. At best they are hearing.

Listening is not easy. It requires energy and stamina of the emotional and intellectual kind. It requires concentration and most of all it requires a genuine interest in what other people have to say.

One of the little things you can do to impress your customers is to listen to them with a pair of sincerely attentive ears. Most people want an audience for their stories and when you provide this they will love you for it. By listening carefully you convince them that their stories are of value and important to you as well as to them. Listening to customers helps raise their self-esteem and furthermore creates the understanding that forms the cornerstone of any meaningful relationship.

Many people don't like listening to customers, for the simple reason that it exposes problems they don't want to hear about. It also diverts time from other activities. As time costs money, why waste money on listening to customers?

However, if you believe that successful business is based on relationships, you have no option but to listen to your customers. Incredible customer service can't be achieved in any other way.

Here are some simple guidelines for listening to customers:

1   To listen effectively you must be genuinely interested in customers and what they have to say.

2   Listen with the sole intention of gaining a deep understanding of customers, of what makes them tick, what they like and dislike, and more specifically their needs and wants in relation to your products and services.

3   Your demeanor, body language, and tone of voice must also reinforce your genuine efforts to listen effectively. We all know when someone is not really listening to us.

4   When listening to customers there are only three reasons for opening your mouth:
    ❖ To ask questions to clarify understanding.
    ❖ To reflect back to customers what they are saying in order to demonstrate understanding.
    ❖ To respond to questions they ask.

5   Effective listening always requires an outcome, such as an action or decision to resolve a problem, meet a need, or help with a purchase. It is important in every conversation with a customer to keep focused on this outcome and thus discreetly steer the conversation to this conclusion.

Nevertheless, there is a limit to listening. Some customers who are lonely and deprived of social contact want to tell their life stories, while others are exceptionally verbose and have the habit of wandering around the countryside before reaching their main point. This can be at the expense of you being able to devote time to other customers who are waiting patiently.

Guideline 5 is important here. This is the subtle skill of politely and deftly steering a conversation to a sensible conclusion that will satisfy a customer, without them feeling rushed and being denied the opportunity of fully expressing themselves.

Listening is an art form and requires the orchestration of many microbehaviors to demonstrate what is really in your heart, that you are genuinely interested in each customer and what he or she wants to say.

BUZZ PRACTICE 37
Focus all your attention on listening carefully to each of your customers so you can end the day understanding them much better.

BUZZ QUOTE
People who never listen think they know everything. People who listen know better.

37

38 INCREASE YOUR PRODUCT KNOWLEDGE

Set at least five minutes aside today to increase your product knowledge.

Product knowledge is essential. The more you know about your products, your stock levels, your services, your company, and your competitors, the more you can do for your customers. There is nothing more frustrating than attempting to purchase a product from someone who knows nothing about it. The more knowledge you have, the more you will have to tap into in order to answer the questions your customers have.

Kevin Burley, a hotel manager, used to run regular quizzes for his staff to help them develop their product knowledge. He would go into the staff rest room and hold an impromptu quiz, asking them questions such as: "We have a special Valentine's dinner promotion coming up. Can you tell me the price and what's on the menu?" In his view, everyone who worked in the hotel should know the answer to such questions. Whether a guest bumped into a member of housekeeping or someone from the back office, it was important that they should have the answer to any question thrown at them.

Byron Taylor, a regional manager with TNT Express in the UK, tells of the "Discover" initiative in which he is involved. TNT teams from all around the UK are invited to compete in a national quiz run along the lines of *Who wants to be a millionaire?* at which groups are tested on their product knowledge, company knowledge, and knowledge of the marketplace. The finals take place in a major convention center, with substantial prices going to the winning team.

Acquiring know-how about products, stock, and your company can thus be made to be fun. A buzz can be created by the whole process. Developing product knowledge should not be a chore but a fascinating experience that enhances the value of each employee and gives benefit to customers.

PRODUCT KNOWLEDGE FUN

✪ Create impromptu product (and stock) knowledge quizzes with prizes (like chocolate bars) for those who score 80 percent or more.

✪ Run product (and stock) knowledge Olympics with gold medals for winners.

✪ Accredit individuals as product knowledge specialists when they have developed sufficient expertise.

✪ Use team meetings to share knowledge on new products.

Many manufacturers work closely with major retailers to train people in the use of their products, whether they be washing machines or lawn mowers. It is to the advantage of everyone involved—the manufacturer, the retailer, and the customer—that store assistants have in-depth knowledge of the products they are selling. The risk otherwise is that promises are made about non-existent features on the equipment or that false indications are given about the capability of the kit, and as a result customers are misled and left dissatisfied.

No matter how much classroom and on-site training a company provides, an individual employee must be motivated to learn about new products and changes. Some large department stores stock over 500,000 different lines with a "churn" of 20 percent a year. This produces immense challenges for front-line people serving customers.

That is why TNT Express gives its Discover quiz the subtitle "The fifth dimension." The fifth dimension of any successful business is to become a learning organization.

BUZZ PRACTICE 38

Develop your expertise every day by learning something new about the products you have in stock and the services you supply.

BUZZ QUOTE

As far as the customer is concerned, you are the expert on the product or service being sold.

38

39 STUDY WORLD-CLASS CUSTOMER SERVICE

It is impossible to deliver world-class service unless you know what it is. You have to study it every day.

Being world-class requires you to push back the boundaries by learning about the best that other practitioners have to offer. It is one of the little things we can do every day, because the lessons are all around us.

The initiative to buzz and become world-class must come from you. It is not sufficient for you to rely on head office executives to define what world-class means and then have the head office training department supply the courses to achieve this. Everyone should be studying customer service. It is like a language—you can improve it all the time.

Fortunately we are immersed in customer service all the time. We are either providing or receiving it. Most days we are subject to customer service experiences that we can reflect on, study, and learn from. The resources available, formal and informal, are immense:

WORLD-CLASS CUSTOMER SERVICE STUDY RESOURCES
- ✪ Your everyday experiences.
- ✪ Visiting establishments that provide world-class service.
- ✪ Experiences of friends and families (through stories they tell of service that buzzes).
- ✪ Customer service books (Amazon.com lists over 51,000 titles on the subject).
- ✪ The internet (Google lists over 9 million entries if you type in "customer service").
- ✪ Discussing customer service with people from other companies and identifying what makes a buzz.
- ✪ Formal training courses (organized by your company).
- ✪ Personal training programs (initiated by you).
- ✪ Daily newspapers (with stories of service).
- ✪ Films and TV (with examples of service).
- ✪ Seeking advice from the experts.
- ✪ Specialist journals.

WORLD-CLASS BUZZ NEWS

In other words, the opportunities to study and learn about customer service are almost infinite. Through a conscious study of world-class service you can constantly learn how to improve. In fact, if you learn and apply one new thing every day through your studies, then in a year you will have learnt and applied 365 new things—and you will be streets ahead of your competitors. You will be up there with those who deliver world-class service.

As a start point in your studies, try to identify one organization that provides world-class service. Then study this organization. Visit it as a customer. Chat to its employees. Take notes and highlight key points. Find out what makes this company buzz so that it consistently delivers high standards of service. Examine its approach and learn from it.

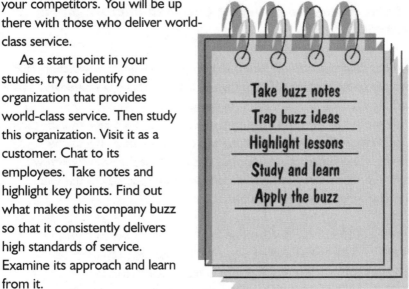

Take buzz notes

Trap buzz ideas

Highlight lessons

Study and learn

Apply the buzz

Then repeat this exercise with other world-class companies. Talk to the experts. Study the books and journals that feature customer service. Learn as you go along and then apply the lessons to yourself, continually asking yourself: "What can I do differently to make things even better for customers and create a buzz?"

BUZZ PRACTICE 39
Prepare a study program for becoming world-class. Draw up a list of resources that you can tap into as part of your studies—and then start learning.

BUZZ QUOTE
Successful people do not confine their studies to the classroom. They are life-long students.

40 CHALLENGE YOURSELF EVERY DAY

Challenge yourself every day: "Am I doing enough to deliver a buzz and improve on my approach?"

Without challenge we fall victim to complacency and arrogance. In our own personal academy of learning we need to challenge ourselves every day: "Am I doing enough, can I do better?"

In pursuit of this challenge, one department of a major retailer came up with the brilliant idea of having a "verb of the day." It was the haberdashery department and they decided that the whole team would challenge themselves to focus on one verb on each day of the week. The following are some examples:

MONDAY	LISTEN	"Our challenge today is to LISTEN to all customers approaching us."
TUESDAY	LEARN	"Our challenge today is to LEARN something about each customer."
WEDNESDAY	HELP	"Our challenge today is to focus on HELPING customers."
THURSDAY	SMILE	"Our challenge today is to SMILE at customers we pass by."
FRIDAY	ENGAGE	"Our challenge today is to ENGAGE customers who are browsing."
SATURDAY	GREET	"Our challenge today is to GREET every approaching customer."
SUNDAY	PRAISE	"Our challenge today is to PRAISE our customers."

Another store in the same group came up with the challenge of converting Saturday into "Chatterday." The idea was simple: Store assistants would be encouraged to chat to as many customers as possible. The store claims that sales increased by 9 percent as a result.

Mandy Givens, a supervisor in an insurance company, invented the game of "verb cards." She took a pack of 52 playing cards and stuck a different verb on the face of each one. On a Friday she would go round her team of claims agents and ask them to select one of the cards from a face-down pack. Their challenge was to put into practice whatever the verb might be. It could be "Care" or "Suggest" or "Personalize." At the end of the shift Mandy reviewed with each team member the extent to which they had been able to apply that particular verb.

Nick Harris, a training officer in a building services company, had a similar idea for his in-house customer service training sessions. He invited groups of participants to select an envelope from a "lucky dip" bucket and then challenged them to perform a role play relating to the verb written on the slip inside the envelope.

Suzanne Cohen, who works in a call center for a telecommunications company, goes through her diary at the start of every month assigning a phrase (such as "warm emotional tone" or "own the customer's problem") to each forthcoming working day. She challenges herself to live up to the phrase when taking calls from customers or making calls to them.

Some team leaders email their people a "quote of the day" to challenge their thinking. Here are just a few:

❖ "Customer service is a specialism—making each customer feel special."
❖ "Every interaction with a customer is an opportunity to create a buzz."
❖ "Trust is the cornerstone of all relationships."
❖ "Those who fail to learn lose out in life's many races."
❖ "If you like a customer the customer will probably like you."
❖ "The most important person is the one you are with now."
❖ "Before you can achieve anything with a customer you have to believe you can."

Set yourself the buzz challenge BUZZ TODAY!

By doing a little thing like selecting a word, verb, phrase, or quote each day you can provide a useful challenge to yourself and your team. It enables you to remain fresh and energized as you focus on applying the verb. It is so easy to relapse into habit and become tired and jaded.

The selected verb also can provide a useful focus for reviewing progress with a team and also in providing training.

BUZZ PRACTICE 40
Start the process today by focusing on the word *buzz*.

BUZZ QUOTE
In the first instance was the word. In the second instance was the behavior that put the word into practice.

THE PSYCHOLOGY OF BUZZ

"It's all in the mind" is a cliché, but it's true. That is where it starts. The little things you do reflect what is in your conscious or subconscious mind. In the latter case we are talking about habits and routines that we don't even think about (for example how to tie a shoelace).

In the former case we are talking about conscious behavioral choices that we make every day when we are with customers. These choices can relate to such little things as whether or not to make eye contact or whether or not to open the door. In the end, it is all to do with psychology, our own and that of customers and colleagues.

We therefore need to work on our attitudes and mindsets in a range of little ways to ensure that we are doing our best for our customers.

41 CREATE THE DRIVE FOR BUZZ

Focus on creating a buzz. Your greatest desire at work should be to please your customers.

"I have fallen in love with Asia," says Julie Mead. She has just returned from Thailand, where she was on honeymoon with Sean, her new husband. She stayed at the Shangri-La Hotel in Bangkok. "Nothing was too much trouble for the people there. They just went out of their way to please us. Their delight seemed to come from delighting us."

For example, Julie has a nut allergy and tells of how one hotel employee went out of his way to describe all the foods on the buffet and explain which did and did not have nuts. He seemed to be genuinely concerned for her. In comparison, she recounts an experience in an expensive and well-known restaurant in London where they did not seem to be bothered about her nut allergy—and as a result she had a severe reaction to a petit four that she innocently ate at the end of the meal.

> One little thing you can do today is to give some serious thought to the question:
>
> "Why do I come to work?"

Customer service that buzzes will never occur unless every single individual in the team genuinely wants it to happen. It relates to the inner drives that motivate people and is something that can't be imposed by bosses with motivation programs. The issue is deep-rooted and begs the question "Why do I come to work?" If the answer is "Simply to earn a living" or "To please my boss," then your priorities need to be reviewed.

The preferred answer is "To ensure that customers have as positive an experience as possible." When the sole aim of everyone in a team is to deliver world-class customer service, the place will buzz. Customers notice it when people try to delight them and they are delighted as a result. They also notice it when there is no effort to please them, when front-line people simply go through the motions.

Customers become alienated by such hypocrisy and lack of genuine endeavor.

When customers are delighted the rest falls into place: employees are motivated, managers reassured, and shareholders satisfied. All other things being equal, it is far better to buy from someone who pleases you than someone who displeases you.

The buzz is thus a function of the spirit and motivational drives of each member of the team. When customers enjoy a world-class service experience, there has been a spirited effort to achieve this. Spirit comes from the soul—and therefore to create a buzz we have to dig deep into our innermost being to determine what drives us forward in life. There is no escaping this. We can't pretend that achieving outstanding service drives us when we really have more selfish aims in mind and have little genuine interest in customers.

Sleep on in it, dwell on it, reflect on it, and spend a little more time today to dig deep into your spirit and determine what your innermost motivational drivers are when it comes to work.

BUZZ PRACTICE 41
Be totally honest with yourself and state here your prime motivational driver at work. If it is not "to deliver world-class customer service," ask yourself why and discuss this with your team and your boss.

BUZZ QUOTE
To deliver world-class customer service there can only be one motivational driver: to provide the most positive experience possible for customers.

42 PREPARE FOR THE BUZZ EVERY DAY

Before you start work every day, prepare your frame of mind to create a buzz.

"I tell myself that today is not just going to be another day but a better day," says Clara Tan, who works at Changi Airport in Singapore. On the way to work, before the start of every shift, one little thing she does is prepare her mind for the work ahead.

Her positive outlook and the way she buzzes are reflected in her attitude and all her behaviors. "Sometimes it's difficult," she added. "We get abuse from passengers, but at the end of the day, if I can serve each of my passengers well with a smile and I've done my best, then he or she will have had the best experience." That is her goal, "To do her best for each customer every day," and it makes her buzz.

FANTASTIC!
It's Monday and I'm going to meet some wonderful customers at work today

You can only make a big difference for customers if you are prepared to make a big difference with every little thing you do every day. And that means preparation. It means preparing your mind to put it in a positive frame before you start work. Negative thoughts need to be flushed away and replaced with exciting thoughts about the day ahead, for example about the interesting new customers whom you will encounter in the coming eight hours and

BAD NEWS
It's Friday and there's no more work for two days

the myriad of opportunities that will be presented to you for pleasing them.

Start each day with some short buzz exercises to create the necessary frame of mind for dealing with customers.

This preparation is essential. You can do it in the shower, sitting in a traffic jam, or as you walk across the car park to the front line where you will be engaging with customers, internal or external. If you don't prepare in this way your mind will drift onto other subjects and there is a risk that you will allow negative thoughts to infect your thinking.

Today is going to be a great day!

Suzette Martell, employee of the year with the retailer ODEL in Colombo, Sri Lanka, listens to cheerful music every morning before coming to work. This gets her into a happy frame of mind to meet her first customer.

In companies that buzz the accent is on the positive. It means creating a positive perspective about all the good things that have happened and will happen during the course of the time we spend at work. It means preparing to be delighted when a customer comes in or calls, or when a customer demands something out of the ordinary—or even something ordinary.

All it takes is one little thought first thing in the morning, for example: "Today is going to be a great day."

BUZZ PRACTICE 42
Every morning before you start work, spend 30 seconds thinking about the customers you will meet during the day and the positive experiences you will provide for them. Every morning spend 30 seconds thinking about how you will create a buzz.

BUZZ QUOTE
You can only make a big difference for customers if you are prepared to make a difference with everything you do every day.

43 KEEP CONSCIOUS

Be conscious of everything that is going on around you.

One of the biggest problems in customer service is that front-line people are frequently not conscious of the customers in their vicinity and what is happening to them.

For example, they are not conscious that:

❖ A customer wants to pay the bill.
❖ Customers have entered the shop.
❖ A line or queue has suddenly formed.
❖ A customer has a need to buy something.
❖ A customer is looking for someone to help her.
❖ A customer is struggling to find the item he wants.
❖ The looks on their own faces have an impact on customers.
❖ Customers are leaving, frustrated in their attempt to obtain service.
❖ A table is dirty and customers are looking for somewhere to sit.
❖ A customer has said something and asked a question.
❖ They are irritating customers by ignoring them.
❖ There is litter on the floor.
❖ The customer is in a rush.

So they do nothing! They either do what they have been told to do or do what they want to do (such as chat to their workmates). What they fail to do is what the customers want them to do—because they are not conscious of what those customers want.

To create buzzing connections, customer consciousness has to be developed and put into practice, applied all the time that customers are around.

Keeping conscious requires little things like having a roving eye, being alert, and detecting when customers require attention. It means having a listening ear and becoming aware of what customers are really saying. It also means being conscious of a customer's tone of voice and emotional state.

By becoming fully conscious of customers, front-line employees can more effectively respond to little things happening around them, for example a customer looking lost or needing help. If they are conscious that a queue has formed, front-line people can either give a sympathetic response—"I'll be with you in a minute"—or take action to get another counter opened.

Consciousness is a skill that can be developed in order to detect opportunities to do something special for a customer. Thus employees will become conscious that a customer is struggling with his bags and will volunteer to take them to the car park for him. They will become conscious that another customer is in a rush and try to complete his transaction as quickly as possible.

Consciousness is a mental process in which people select signals on which they believe action is required. We tend not to be conscious of things that are unimportant to us. Consciousness is therefore driven by our values. If customers and their wellbeing are really important to us, we need to become conscious of a customer's every need so that we can take action to generate that wellbeing.

BUZZ PRACTICE 43
Look out for customers.
Look out for customers requiring help.
Look out for opportunities to please customers.
Look out for things to do that please customers.
By looking out we keep conscious.

BUZZ QUOTE
If they are fully conscious of customers front-line employees can be much more effective.

43

44 TAKE RISKS WITH YOUR CUSTOMERS

No risk, no buzz. Take a risk and push back the boundaries to achieve world-class service.

Too many companies are risk averse, suffering the illusion that no risks need to be taken en route to success. Mediocrity results as people follow the same old procedures, supposedly formulated and unwisely adopted for maximum gain. But there is no gain from such formulae. Success is synonymous with risk.

The key question is: "Who takes the risk?" In bureaucratic organizations nobody does except senior executives. Everything is referred up to the top floor. Empowerment does not exist and people at the front line feel unable to take risky decisions that effectively deviate from the norm of rules and procedures.

Conversely, in companies that buzz risks are taken by front-line people. They feel able (and thus enabled) to break the rules in favor of a customer, even though there is always a risk that this will backfire.

To create a buzz it is essential to pick up little signals from customers and then take risks in responding to them as best you can:

- ✔ Risk calling a customer by his first name.
- ✔ Risk approaching a grumpy-looking customer.
- ✔ Risk a comment on a customer's new hairstyle.
- ✔ Risk stepping outside routine to help a customer.
- ✔ Risk suggesting a second purchase to the customer.
- ✔ Risk making a joke when you are unsure of the response.
- ✔ Risk taking an extra ten minutes to solve a customer's problem.
- ✔ Risk spending $50 to compensate a customer for all the hassle.
- ✔ Risk asking a personal question such as "How did you meet your wife?"
- ✔ Risk breaking the rules by opening the office ten minutes early for a customer.
- ✔ Risk sending the customer some flowers (or a bottle of wine) at company expense.
- ✔ Risk overruling your boss in favor of a customer if you believe the decision is right.

In one hotel group, staff were instructed not to shake hands with guests on arrival as it was felt this would alienate female guests from certain countries. Furthermore, the management did not want every employee guests encountered shaking hands with them as they walked through the hotel. The overall impact of this instruction was to create a rather distant and impersonal service. It would have been far better if the staff had been advised on when and when not to shake hands and exercising the risk had then been left to their discretion.

Every simple piece of behavior can carry a risk of offending a customer. As a result, front-line people often shy away from taking such behavioral risks. They do not offer hands for shaking, they do not make eye contact, they do not approach customers, they do not ask questions—all for the simple reason that there is a faint risk that these initiatives might cause offense.

Little risks can lead to BIG satisfaction

If you minimize risky behavior, customer service becomes minimalistic. The minimalistic view is that it is far better to approach no customers than to approach ten and risk upsetting the four who do not wish to be approached.

The same applies to giving things to customers. The risk is that if you give something to one customer you risk upsetting the one you do not give it to. So in the end nobody receives a complimentary coffee—unless everyone is offered it. By minimizing risk we tend toward the lowest common denominator of mediocrity, predictability, and a total absence of buzz.

To create a buzz you have to take little risks frequently. You have to play music when the risk is that customers want a quiet time. You have to be proactive in initiating contact when the risk is that all customers want is a passive response.

BUZZ PRACTICE 44
Take a risk today and push the boundaries of your own behavior. Approach and chat to people you don't normally chat to. Give away things you don't normally give away. Do something creative and risk rejection.

BUZZ QUOTE
Failure to take a risk will result in failure.

44

45 APPLY COMMON SENSE

Use common sense today—nothing works better.

So much of customer service is common sense that it is surprising that evidence of it is so uncommon. It is common sense to find time for customers and respond to their requirements—yet frequently it does not happen.

It is common sense to make customers feel good, to listen to them and understand their needs. It is common sense to do everything possible to help customers and ensure that they have the most positive experience possible (that's the buzz). Yet it rarely happens, for the simple reason that many companies, many managers, and many front-line people take leave of their common sense. They forget what service is all about, being totally preoccupied with task and profit rather than being obsessed with the people who hand over the money to them.

It is common sense to:
- ✪ Say thank you.
- ✪ Smile at customers.
- ✪ Welcome customers.
- ✪ Show good manners.
- ✪ Build relationships with customers.
- ✪ Apologize when something goes wrong.
- ✪ Keep customers informed.

Is it common sense:
- ✘ To keep a customer waiting?
- ✘ Not to answer the phone?
- ✘ To ignore a customer?
- ✘ Not to call back as promised?
- ✘ To allow a frustrated customer to walk out of the door?

Before writing this section I undertook a short experimental mystery shopping survey. I entered ten different establishments, ranging from a bank, a betting shop, and a bakery to a leisure center, a department store, and a supermarket, as well as a chemist, a coffee shop, and a travel agent. In each establishment I was potentially a new customer, yet in none of them was I welcomed. I was ignored and not a single employee attempted to build a relationship with me. When I eventually got to each counter the front-line people merely did the task: They supplied the information, processed the transaction, and packaged the product as appropriate. No one attempted to discover my name, let alone call me by it. The communication that took place was mechanical and routine. There was no buzz in any of these places and therefore no real reason for me to return.

The problem with common sense is that it is frequently not applied. We all get into bad habits and forget to say thank you, or neglect to call customers by their names, or simply ignore them when we have something else on our mind.

The challenge in creating the buzz is to challenge common sense and then apply it. It is common sense not to smoke, but a big challenge to give it up. It is common sense not to drink too much alcohol, but a big challenge to restrict our consumption to one or two glasses. It is common sense not to eat too much, but a big challenge to resist that incredibly attractive dessert. It is common sense to take a regular amount of exercise, but a big challenge to find the time and energy to do so.

Is there a better way?

Creating a buzz is common sense, but it requires the challenge of applying many of the basic behaviors that we well know are important but that we are in danger of neglecting as the pressures of daily life take over. It is common sense to give a customer everything we possibly can, but much easier to do the bare minimum. It is common sense to take an interest in a customer, to listen to them intently, and to explore their needs with a view to meeting them, but it is far easier to concentrate our attention on simple routines that demand less of our energy.

It does not take miracles or even magic to create a buzz, it just takes a lot of common sense and focusing all our creative energies and hard work on making a customer feel special.

BUZZ PRACTICE 45
When you are unsure of something you are doing, stop and ask yourself: "Is this common sense? Is there a better way?"

BUZZ POINT
Common sense has to be challenged to be applied. 45

THE FINAL FIVE

The buzz is a reflection of all the choices a team makes. When people are in automatic mode there is no choice, they just act in accordance with preprogrammed instructions. They behave like robots. Such a mechanized approach can never lead to a buzz.

Every interaction with a customer presents you with a choice. You can choose to transcend the routine in order to make the interaction a high-quality, world-class experience, or you can choose merely to follow the routine and make the interaction ordinary.

The number of options from which you can choose is infinite. For example, there is an infinite number of ways you can converse with a customer, make suggestions, listen to them, and sound out ideas.

Here is a final set of five little things you can choose to do that will make a big difference in delivering world-class service to your customers.

46 PRAISE CUSTOMERS

Challenge yourself to find an occasion to praise a customer today.

Maria Rincon was trying on a hat in Peter Jones department store in Sloane Square in London. The only store assistant available, Drusilla, was serving another customer. She caught Maria's eye and signaled that she would be with her in a minute. Drusilla was as good as her word. As she approached Maria she looked at her with admiration: "Madam, you do look so beautiful in that hat."

Drusilla is one of the wonderful "partners" who work for the John Lewis company. The way she praised Maria was totally genuine. It came from her heart.

At a restaurant in the Castle Hotel in Windsor the waitress praised me for my choice of main course, saying that it was her favorite too. For some reason I enjoyed the meal more knowing that my selection had the waitress's approval.

It is so easy to praise customers, yet few of us seize the opportunity to do so. Here are some further examples:

- ✪ "I really like that aftershave you're wearing. If you don't mind me asking, what is it?"
- ✪ "I am full of admiration, your children are so well behaved."
- ✪ "I am absolutely convinced you have made the right decision."
- ✪ "I am impressed by your attitude on this issue."
- ✪ "You really do look smart in your new suit."
- ✪ "You look well today."
- ✪ "I love your new hairstyle."
- ✪ "I must praise your knowledge of this subject."
- ✪ "You are very wise. It would be better to leave this purchase for another time."
- ✪ "I really appreciate you bringing back this piece of equipment. We do need to know when our products are not working properly."

Praising customers (as well as colleagues, managers, employees, and other people) is a "heartset" that all of us need to acquire and sustain during our lives. The use of praise puts a relationship on a positive footing and facilitates a warm, friendly interaction when serving customers. In turn, customers will perceive this as incredible customer service—for the simple reason that they rarely receive praise from other people.

There are some simple guidelines when it comes to praising customers:

- The praise must be original and specific.
- The praise must always be sincere and genuine.
- It must be spontaneous (and never engineered or routine).
- There are opportunities to praise customers every working day.
- Praise can even extend to flattery should you judge the situation suitable.
- Praise must not be overdone. It must be reserved for something special.

What are your lines of praise?

With respect to flattery, there is no harm is using it in moderation, for example in saying to a senior citizen who is full of energy, "How do you keep so young?"

The practice of praise should also extend to internal service and anyone from within your team or another department who is helpful. Never hesitate to praise—everyone welcomes it, including your boss, your director, and all your colleagues.

To praise people is easy. It simply means going out of the way each day to look for the good things in other people. As soon as you start looking you will find them and then the praise will come naturally.

BUZZ PRACTICE 46
Study your customers (internal and external) carefully and identify at least one thing about one of them today that is worthy of praise. Then come up with some choice words with which to praise them.

BUZZ QUOTE
Any customer who does business with you needs to be praised.

46

USE NAMES

The best way to personalize a relationship with customers is to use their names. Ensure that you mention the customer's name in every conversation.

There is a certain restaurant that Dianne Colley, an American executive coach, visits where the head waiter always opens the door and greets her by name. Simple, isn't it? How often do you visit an establishment a second or third time and the people there know your name?

It is one of the accepted practices of modern customer service that front-line people should use customers' names—yet few do. The information about customers' names is invariably available: for example on the boarding pass for a flight, on the paying-in slip at the bank, on a credit card, on a passport, on the reservations list, and on a registration form. The opportunities for using a customer's name are endless but rarely taken up.

Customer No. 150374 Mrs Hannah

And even if the information is not there, it is not difficult to ask: "My name is Theresa, I'm afraid I didn't catch your name." Most customers are happy to provide their names in such circumstances.

As soon as customers' names are discovered they should be used. It creates a real buzz. In studies of psychology and motivation, it has been well established for many years that a customer's esteem is enhanced when they hear their own name. It makes them feel important. Furthermore, when their name is connected with the name of the person they are dealing with, the relationship is strengthened further. It works both ways.

Cecilia Estrop, a customer service agent at Changi Airport, Singapore, loves helping customers who encounter problems. Their flights might have been delayed, their bags might have been lost or damaged, or they simply might not have been assigned the seat they wanted with extra legroom. Often these customers are very angry and

Cecilia's first encounter will be with a person who is on the verge of losing his or her temper. Her first step is to introduce herself by name, hand the customer her name card, and then establish the customer's name, if she does not know it already. The use of names in this way creates a relationship bond that facilitates the resolution of what can be a difficult problem.

Discretion and sensitivity are required in testing out whether or not to use titles. Should it be Mr. Confrey or Roger Confrey? The transition from the formal to the informal is a difficult barrier to cross and has to be tested. If in doubt, the wise thing is to err on the side of formality and call the customer Mr. Confrey as opposed to Roger. If you are unlikely to see the customer again, it is best to be formal. However, if you anticipate that this customer will be a regular then there is no harm in enquiring: "How would you like to be addressed, Mr. Confrey or Roger?" The majority of customers will prefer the latter, the informality enhancing the relationship and adding value to it.

Acquiring, remembering, and using names is a basic but an essential challenge in delivering world-class customer service that buzzes.

BUZZ PRACTICE 47

Play the name game, perhaps with your colleagues. Draw two columns on a blank piece of paper, the left-hand column headed "Regulars" and the right-hand column headed "New customers." At the end of the day (or at the start of the next day), list the names of the customers that you can recall having met that day.

BUZZ POINT
The more customers you can name personally,
the better your service provision will be.

48 UNDERTAKE GOOD DEEDS

Be good to customers by choosing to undertake good deeds for them. It will be good for you too.

99.99 percent of people in this world are good. Everyone wants to be good. They want to be good to you and they want you to be good to them. Choosing to do good deeds is the natural consequence of such goodness. Most people like to do good deeds. It creates a real buzz.

When it comes to service, a good deed is going beyond the routine for customers. A good deed therefore cannot be defined in a job description or prescribed by a manager. Good deeds are those little extra things that you genuinely want to do for customers. A good deed comes from you, not from anyone else. As soon as you instruct another person, say an employee, to undertake a good deed, it ceases to be so, it becomes a task assigned by another person.

Here are some examples of good deeds:

✪ When a caller mentioned that her son was ill, the call center agent rang back a day later to find out how the boy was.

✪ A call center agent discovered that one of her customers was about to get married, so she sent her a card.

✪ A customer mentioned in passing to a call center agent that she was interested in homeopathy, so the agent sent her a newspaper cutting on the subject.

✪ A woman calling about her telephone account proudly told the call center agent that she was about to become a grandmother. So the agent gave her a £2 ($4) credit, because he knew she would be making a few more calls when the happy event happened.

✪ A call center agent sent a customer a handwritten personal letter of apology when informed of some mammoth screw-up made by her company.

✪ A store assistant entertained a child to stop him screaming.

✪ A receptionist helped with an old man in a wheelchair, pushing it across the lobby for his wife.

✪ A team of credit controllers at Rand Air, Wadeville, South Africa call customers who pay early to say "thank you."

A key factor in the way customers judge your service is the good deeds you do. They will take the normal things, like processing the transaction efficiently, for granted and will not comment on this. However, they will like you for your good deeds, for the thought you put into doing some little extra good deed to please a customer. It does not take much, except perhaps some good thinking in the first place.

A good deed might simply be a few words of sympathy followed by a card or offering to deliver an urgently required item personally to a customer's home. In a leather goods shop, I saw an assistant offer the use of her own cellphone to a customer who was trying to call her husband and had found that the battery on her phone was flat.

Opening doors for customers, escorting them to the entrance when saying goodbye, and offering to carry their bags are all good deeds.

When was the last time you did a good deed for a customer?

BUZZ PRACTICE 48
Become a good deed pioneer in your company. Challenge yourself to undertake one good deed every day.

BUZZ QUOTE
Never expect anything in return for a good deed. As soon as you do, it ceases to be a good deed and becomes a transaction.

49 MAKE PROMISES AND KEEP THEM

The more promises you make to customers, the more you will keep your customers. Go out and promise something now.

Customers judge you by the little promises you make and keep, as well as the big ones. If you make no promises it is unlikely that you will keep your customers, for the simple reason that it is promises that bind you to them. Promises are a token of the essential trust that needs to be established between people. When promises are broken that trust is eroded. When there are no promises there can be no trust.

Thus in any relationship with a customer it is important to make promises—and to keep them. These promises can be little things you plan to do for customers or even bigger things. Choosing to promise something gives you an opportunity to demonstrate that you are there for the customer and that you are dedicating your top priority to meeting their needs and expectations.

Here are some examples of promises you can make to a customer:

❖ "I will be with you in a minute."
❖ "I will get back to you by Friday."
❖ "I will call you within ten minutes."
❖ "I will chase up the suppliers and make sure it is delivered by Monday at the latest."
❖ "This is going to take a few weeks, but I will definitely keep you advised of progress."
❖ "If there is any problem with this purchase please ring me personally and I will ensure that it is replaced immediately."
❖ "I will drop by in three months' time to see how you are getting along with this new machine."
❖ "I confess I'm not an expert on this issue. I'll make sure that Ismail Waheed, our technical specialist, rings you within 24 hours to advise you."
❖ "I can assure you that we can serve you a two-course lunch within an hour."
❖ "I'll sort this problem out for you, don't worry. I'll let you know when it's fixed."

In each of the above examples there is an implicit promise that must be kept. If you say you will call back in a minute, you must do so. If you say you are going to drop by in three months' time, equally you must do so.

Do not make promises you are unsure you can keep, for example "I can promise you your wife will be absolutely delighted with this gift" (especially if you don't know the customer's wife) or "If you visit our leisure park we can promise you a good time" (which might not happen if the weather is poor and the kids are screaming).

This is my promise to you, the customer

It is important to differentiate between an output and an outcome. You can rarely promise an outcome, while you can promise an output. Thus for a vacation you cannot promise a great time (an outcome), but you can promise great service (an output). If a customer is ill on vacation a great time will not be had, even though the customer can benefit from the promised great service.

In creating the buzz the skill is to seek out opportunities as frequently as possible to make promises and then to keep them. In doing so you are generating commitments and positive behaviors that bind you to customers. These behaviors reassure customers and give them the confidence to deal with you personally again. By making and keeping promises, you create the trust that is essential to all relationships.

BUZZ PRACTICE 49
Make a mental and written note of every promise you make and then keep them.

BUZZ QUOTE
The buzz is all about attracting customers to your
company, with the promise of world-class service.
Make that promise every day and keep it.

50 SUGGEST AS MUCH AS A CUSTOMER CAN TAKE

Never underestimate the power of suggestion in delivering outstanding service. Add value with your suggestions.

Mid-afternoon in a little Parisian brasserie, the chef emerges from the kitchen with a tray of steaming hot tarte au citron. As they drink their café crèmes, he presents the tray to each customer and gestures to them, suggesting they have a portion. Most of the customers are tempted and nod. No words are spoken. With a few simple gestures of suggestion an additional 50 euros of revenue is taken.

A customer visited Austin Reed in Regent Street, London to purchase a new suit for a forthcoming wedding. After he had selected the suit, the assistant suggested that he acquire a new shirt and tie along with a new pair of shoes: "You can't go to a wedding with an old shirt, let alone wear a three-year-old tie and an ancient pair of shoes." It was all part of the service and of course resulted in add-on sales of approximately 20 percent.

At another branch of the same chain, a customer saw some short-sleeved shirts displayed in the window. He entered the shop to express an interest in the shirts. "Are you going somewhere hot?" the assistant asked. "I'm going to Saudi Arabia," replied the customer. "You are going to need a lightweight suit there," suggested the assistant, "have you got one?" "No, I plan to take my normal suit." "We have a brand new range of lightweight suits just come in. I would suggest you take a look at them." And of course a lightweight suit was purchased, even though the intention had only been to buy a short-sleeved shirt.

Another example is a coffee shop in Windsor. When customers come in and ask for a cappuccino, the baristas will invariably suggest a large one unless the customer specifies otherwise (small or regular). They will also suggest a fresh muffin to accompany the cappuccino.

There is nothing immoral or devious about suggesting to customers additional purchases to meet their requirements. In fact, in most cases it helps them. One store assistant with a major retailer comments, "Customers can get very upset, having bought a new laptop, if they get home and found they have not bought the accessories they require, for example backup devices."

Suggestion is akin to proactive advice. It helps. Customers are as forgetful and indulgent as the rest of us and sometimes it requires no more than a little nudge of suggestion to take them down a route that they will appreciate. The suggestion does not always have to be linked directly to additional sales, but can relate to anything that enhances and benefits the customer. It might be that a cashier at the bank carrying out a foreign exchange transaction discovers that the customer is visiting Cape Town for the first time and suggests that she visit Hermanus to see whales in their natural surroundings. Or it might be that the insurance consultant discovers that the customer loves fado music and suggests the latest album by Mariza.

Choosing to make suggestions amounts to passing on nuggets of expertise that customers will value. It all adds to the total experience and the buzz that is created. It requires you to discover what is important to customers and then to pass on some new, additional information and advice. It might be suggesting the latest book by Monica Ali to a customer who is interested in ethnic diversity and the cultural dimensions of modern life, or suggesting she see the Indian movie *Monsoon Wedding* or go to the show *Bombay Dreams*.

This works both ways too. Those who revel in making suggestions should equally be amenable to receiving suggestions from customers, whether they relate to changes in opening hours or amendments to the product offering and service delivered.

Suggestion is all about helping others seize opportunities to enhance their lives.

BUZZ PRACTICE 50
Challenge yourself to make one suggestion to at least every tenth customer.

BUZZ QUOTE
Things will buzz when you only
suggest the best for a customer.

50